CAKES
Cupcakes
Coffee cake

APPLE TURNOVERS: TASTY DUTCH TREAT

Sift together: 2 c. all purpose flour, ½ tsp. salt
2 tsp. baking powder, 1/8 tsp. cinnamon
Cut ¾ c. shortening into this.
Add just enough milk to moisten (approximately 5½ tbsp.) toss lightly to form a ball of dough, and roll ¼ inch thick into a rectangle.
Cut into 6 5 inch squares and place 1 peeled, sliced tart apple in center of each square. Sprinkle each sliced apple with 1 tablespoon light brown sugar, a dash of cinnamon, and a dash of nutmeg; dot with butter. Fold corners to make a triangle, pressing edges together with tines of a fork. Arrange on a cookie sheet, ½ inch apart and place in 450° oven. Immediately reduce heat to 375°. Bake 35-40 minutes or until golden brown as pie crust. Can use other fruit or thickened fruit juice, cherry, blueberry, etc.

APPLE CAKE

1 c. sugar	1½ c. flour	¼ tsp. salt
1 tsp. soda	½ c. shortening	1 egg
½ c. milk	1 tsp. vanilla	4 med. diced apples

Mix all together and bake in a loaf pan.

Topping

2 tbsp. butter	½ c. brown sugar	1 tsp. cinnamon
2 tbsp. flour	½ c. nuts	

Put on top and bake at 350° for 45 min.

FRESH APPLE CAKE

2 c. sugar	1½ c. cooking oil
2 eggs	2 tsp. vanilla

Mix and add 3 c. chopped apples.
Combine:

3 c. flour	1 tsp. soda
1 tsp. salt	1 tsp. cinnamon

Mix all ingredients well, makes a stiff batter. Add one cup nuts and bake 30 to 40 min. at 350°.

Reprinted in Loving Memory of our mother
Ada K. Schwartz

the original cover art
as it was
printed in 1972

Amish Recipes

Old and New

Compiled by
ADA K. SCHWARTZ

INTRODUCTION

I hope the readers of this book will find it both useful as well as interesting. I do not claim that the recipes in this book are better than yours, but many do have Amish "variations" which you may find delightful. You will find many different kinds of recipes, many of which were donated by friends and relatives from near and far.

My sincere thanks to them all for their time and help and also for the ladies who helped type, and all who helped in any way in making this book a success. Much time was spent in preparing this book, which I enjoyed. I have been thinking of writing a book of this type for quite some time. And despite all efforts to avoid mistakes, do not be alarmed if you do find some and I hope you will excuse them.

My husband, Dave Y. Schwartz, was killed in an auto accident on October 24, 1970, leaving me with 9 children, ages (now) 11 to 2. Their names are, LuCinda, Emma, Katie, Lydia, David, Elizabeth, Johnny, Samuel and Crist.

The Author
Ada K. Schwartz

MEASURES OFTEN USED

A few grains = less than 1/8 tsp.
Speck = less than 1/8 tsp.
Pinch = as much as can be taken between tip of fingers and thumb.

3 tsp. = 1 tbsp.
4 tbsp. = ¼ cup
16 tbsp. = 1 cup
5 tbsp. + 1 tsp. = 1/3 cup
8 oz. = 1 cup
1 oz. = 2 tbsp. fat or liquid
2 cups fat = 1 lb.

2 cups = 1 pt.
2 pts. = 1 Qt.
2 cups sugar = 1 lb.
2 2/3 cups powder suger = 1 lb.
2 2/3 cups brown sugar = 1 lb.
1 lb. butter = 2 cups or 4 sticks

ABBREVIATIONS USED IN THIS BOOK

Cup	c.
Ounce	oz.
Pound	lb.
Teaspoon	tsp.
Tablespoon	tbsp.
Gallon	gal.
Quart	qt.
Pint	pt.
Dozen	doz.
Large	lge.
Square	sq.
Package	pkg.

AVERAGE CONTENTS OF CANS

8 oz.	1 cup
No. 300	1¾ cup
No. 1 tall	2 cups
No. 303	2 cups
No. 2	2½ cups
No. 2½	3½ cups
No. 3	4 cups

SPICY APPLESAUCE CAKE

1¾ c. sifted cake flour		½ tsp. salt
1 tsp. soda	2 tsp. cinamon	1 tsp. ground cloves
1 tbsp. instant coffee		½ c. shortening
1 c. sugar	1 tsp. vanilla	1 egg
½ c. buttermilk	½ c. applesauce	

Grease bottom of an 8 x 12 inch cake pan. Sift flour, salt, soda, cinnamon, cloves and coffee. Cream shortening and sugar till light and fluffy. Add vanilla and egg and mix well. Combine buttermilk and applesauce, and add alternately with dry ingredients, to the creamed mixture. Pour in pan and bake at 350° for 30 minutes. This is delicious frosted with a brown sugar icing.

CARROT CAKE

2 cups sugar	2 cups flour	2 tsp. baking soda
2 tsp. cinnamon	1 tsp. salt	1¼ c. oil
4 eggs	3 c. grated carrots	

Sift dry ingredients in large bowl. Add oil, eggs and carrots, mix well. If too thick, add a little water to batter. Bake at 350° till done. Ice with favorite icing. Note: Add 2 tablespoons cocoa instead of spice for a Chocolate Carrot Cake. —Mrs. John A. Wenger, Pa.

CARROT CAKE

Sift together:
2 c. flour   2 tsp. baking powder   1½ tsp. soda
2 tsp. cinnamon   1 tsp. salt

Mix 1½ c. salad oil with 2 c. sugar. Add 4 eggs, one at a time, beating after each one. Add dry ingredients and mix well. Add 2 c. grated fine carrots and 1 small can of crushed pineapple and ½ c. chopped nuts. Bake at 350°. Good with cream cheese icing.

CHEESE CAKE

First chill 1 large can Pet milk. Add 1 tsp. vanilla. Whip it. Add 1 cup hot water in Lemon Royal Jello, let stand to thicken. Roll 30 Graham crakers, add 1 stick melted oleo. Take fork, mix it. ½ lb. Phil. Cheese (soft). Mix Phil. Cheese with 1 c. sugar. Add Jello to cheese mixture and mix real good. Then add mixture to whipped milk and mix real good. Put crumbs in two 8 in. cake pans. Put crumbs on top of cheese cake too.
— R.B.S., Berne, Ind.

CHEESE CAKE

1 pkg. lemon Jello
2 tbsp. lemon juice
1 c. sugar
1 lge. can very cold Carnation milk, whipped
1 No. 2 can pineapple   ½ c. melted butter
36 graham crackers.
1 c. boiling water
1 8 oz. pkg. Philadelphia C.C.
1 tbsp. vanilla

Cream sugar, cheese and vanilla. Add Jello and mix well. Fold whipped cream in Jello and mix well. Fold whipped cream in Jello in mixture, then add pineapple and stir. Crush crackers fine and add melted butter. Firmly pack 2/3 of mix in bottom and sides of a large baking dish and add filling and sprinkle with rest of crumbs and chill for several hours.

FRENCH CHERRY CAKE

1 lb. graham crackers, crushed very fine
¾ c. butter, melted   2 tbsp sugar
2 pkgs. Dream Whip   1½ c. powdered sugar
2 8oz. pkgs. Philadelphia Cream cheese
2 cans cherry pie filling.

Mix cracker crumbs, melted butter and 2 tbsp. sugar together. Press into bottom of 13 x 19 x 2 inch pan. Bake at 350° for about 8 minutes. Set aside to cool. Mix package of Dream Whip as directed on box. Mix powdered sugar with cream cheese which has been softened to room temperature. Blend whipped mixture into creamed cheese mixture. Spread over cracker crust and top with cherry pie filling or pineapple. If you use pineapple you need to thicken it. This can be made the day before serving.
—Mrs. Daniel C. Schwartz

CHOCOLATE CHIP BROWNIES

2 c. brown sugar 2 c. flour ½ tsp. soda,
pinch of salt 1 tsp. baking powder
½ c. butter or oleo 2 eggs.
1 tsp. vanilla 1 c. choc. chips 1 c. nuts

Melt butter, pour over sugar, mix. Add eggs and mix. Add flour and dry ingredients and nuts. Spread in buttered pan. Sprinkle chips on top, bake in a moderate oven till lightly browned. Butterscotch chips can be used.
—Mrs. N. N. Miller, Topeka, Ind.

CHOCOLATE SHEET CAKE

Sift together in a bowl 2 c. flour, 2 c. sugar, melt together and bring to a brisk boil 2 sticks Oleo, 2 heaping tbsp. cocoa and 1 c. water. Pour over dry ingredients. Mix and add to above mixture ½ c. buttermilk, 1 tsp. soda, ½ tsp. salt, 1 tsp. vanilla and 2 eggs slightly beaten. Pour on a greased cookie sheet and bake 20 min. only at 350°. — M.S.

CHOCOLATE CHIP CAKE

1¾ c. sifted flour 2 tbsp. cocoa 1 tsp. salt
1 tsp. baking soda 1 cup boiling water
1 c. shortening 1 c. sugar 2 eggs, beaten
1 tsp. vanilla 6 oz. choc. chips ¾ c. chopped nuts

Sift together flour, cocoa, salt and soda. Cream shortning and sugar. Add eggs and vanilla. Beat thoroughly. Add water and flour alternately mixing until smooth after each addition. Spread in greased 13" x 9" pan. Sprinkle top with chips and nuts. Bake in moderate oven 350° for 45 minutes. This may be served with whipped cream. ——Sarah H. Schwartz

CHOCOLATE CAKE WITHOUT EGGS

2 c. br. sugar ½ c. lard ¼ c. chocolate
1 c. milk 1 tsp. salt 2½ c. flour
1 tsp. soda + ½ c. water (strong) Vanilla

Bake at 350° for 25 to 35 minutes.
———Esther Lanbright

COCOA CAKE WITH SOUR CREAM

3 eggs	1½ cups sugar	3 tbsp. cocoa
¼ c. salt	2 c. flour	1 tsp. vanilla
2 tsp. soda	1½ c. sour cream	

Beat eggs well, add sugar, salt and cocoa. Sift together, add soda, dissolve in a little hot water. Sift flour 3 times and add alternating with cream and vanilla. Mix throughly and bake in moderate oven until done.

SUN GOLD COCONUT CAKE

2 c. sugar	1 c. butter	4 eggs
1 c. milk	1 c. coconut	3 c. flour
3 tsp. baking powder		1 tsp. vanilla
pinch of salt	Add egg whites last of all.	

COFFEE CAKE

2½ c. flour	2 c. br. sugar	½ tsp. salt
2/3 c. shortening	2 tsp. baking pow.	½ tsp. cinnamon
½ tsp. nutmeg	½ tsp. soda	1 c. sour milk
2 eggs beaten		

Rub flour, sugar, salt and shortening to fine crumbs. Remove ½ cup of crumb mixture to sprinkle over top. To remaining crumb mixture add baking powder, soda and spices, mixing well. Add milk and eggs and stir until smooth. Pour in pan and sprinkle with ½ c. crumbs, 1/3 c. nuts and ½ tsp. cinnamon. Bake and serve warm.

Mrs. Milo Y. Schwartz

COFFEE CAKE

1½ c. sugar	1 tsp. cinnamon	¾ c. lard
½ tsp. nutmeg	1 c. cold strong coffee	
1 tsp. soda	2½ c. cake flour	2 tsp. baking pow.
2 eggs	add ½ c. raisins if desired.	

Mix sugar, lard and eggs and beat well. Sift dry ingredients and add alternately with coffee to lard, sugar and eggs.

"Cookin' don't last——kisses do."

KLEINA KAFFEE KUCHEN

1 pkg. active dry yeast	¼ c. warm water
½ c. butter or other shortening	3 tbsp. sugar
2 eggs 2 egg yolks	2 c. sifted flour
½ tsp. salt ½ c. cream	

Soften yeast in warm water (let stand 5 to 10 min.). Cream butter until soft, add sugar and cream until fluffy. Add eggs and yolks one at a time. Stir in ½ c. flour and salt. Mix in yeast. Alternately add the remaining flour and the cream to yeast mixture, mixing well after each addition. Grease and flour 12 muffin pan wells. Spoon in dough to half full. Cover, set pans in a warm place until dough is doubled, about 30 min. Bake at 400° about 12 min. Makes 1 doz. individual coffee cakes.

CRUMB CAKE

2 c. br. sugar	2 eggs	½ c. sho
2 tsp. baking pow.	2½ c. flour	1 tsp. so
1 c. thick sour milk		1 tsp. vanilla

Mix sugar, flour, shorening, baking powder and soda together. Then take out 1 cup of crumbs for on top. Mix remaining ingredients and add cinnamon & nutmeg if desired.

KRUM KUCHEN (CRUMB CAKE)

4 c. sifted flour	2 c. sugar	4 tsp. baking pow.
½ tsp. salt	1 c. butter	1 c. milk
4 eggs, separated	¼ c. melted butter	2 tsp. ground cinn.

Sift the first four ingredients together. Cut in butter with a pastry blender until pieces are the size of rice kernals. Measure 1 cup of the crumbs and set aside for topping. Beat egg ylks until thick and add with milk to remaining crumb mixture; stir just until dry ingredients are moistened. Beat the egg whites until rounded peaks are formed. Fold into egg yolk mixture until blended. Turn batter into 2 well greased (bottoms only) 9 x 9 x 2½ inch pans and sprinkle top of each with half of the reserved crumbs. Bake at 375° 20 to 25 minutes. After baking, sprinkle top of each cake with half of a butter-cinnamon mixture.

FILLING FOR CUPCAKES

2/3 c. boiled milk, let cool to lukewarm
½ c. butter   1/3 c. shortening   1 c. white sugar
1 egg white   1½ tsp. vanilla

    Cream butter and shortening, then add sugar a little at a time until creamy. Add egg white and vanilla. Then add lukewarm milk and cream until smooth. Put filling in cookie press and put in the middle of the cupcake. They should be cold before filling. ——Mary Ann Troyer, Apple Creek, Ohio

DATE AND NUT CAKE

2 c. dates, cut up   Pour 2 c. boiling water over dates, cool. Mix: 1 c. shortening, 2 c. white sugar, 2 tsp. vanilla, 2 eggs. After this is all well beaten, sift: 3½ c. flour, 2 tsp. soda, and ½ tsp. salt. Alternate sifted ingredients and dates and water with the rest of batter. Add 1 c. chopped nuts. Bake at 350° to 375° about one hour.

DEVILS FOOD CAKE

1½ c. sugar   1 c. milk   ½ c. shortening
3 eggs separated   2 c. flour   4 tbsp. cocoa
¼ tsp. salt   1 tbsp. vinegar   1½ tsp. soda

    Mix in order given, add beaten egg whites last.

FRUIT COCKTAIL CAKE

1½ c. sugar   2 c. flour   2 eggs
pinch of salt   1½ tsp. soda   1 c. fruit cocktail
1 tsp. vanilla

    Mix dry ingredients. Add fruit cocktail and eggs and vanilla. Stir up with a spoon until mixed good. Bake at 350° 35 to 40 minutes.

HICKORY NUT CAKE

2 c. sugar   ¾ c. Crisco   3 eggs
2¾ c. flour   2 tsp. baking powder
1 tsp. vanilla   ¾ c. nut meats   1 c. milk

    "Too soon ve get oldt, und too late schmardt"

HAPPINESS CAKE

1 c. good thoughts	1 c. kind deeds
1 c. consideration for others	2 c. sacrifice
2 c. well beaten faults	3 c. forgiveness

    Mix thoroughly, add tears of joy, sorrow, and sympathy. Flavor with love and kindly service. Fold in 4 c. of prayer and faith. Blend well. Fold into daily life. Bake well with the warmth of human kindness and serve with a smile anytime. It will satisfy the hunger of starved souls.
    ——Mrs. John Henry Yoder, Virginia Beach, Va.

LEMON "CAKE" DESSERT

½ c. flour	2 c. sugar	1 tsp. salt
6 egg yolks, beaten	½ c. lemon juice	3 c. milk
6 egg whites, stiffly beaten.		

    Sift flour, sugar and salt. Blend egg yolks, lemon juice and milk. Combine liquid and dry ingredients. Beat till smooth. Fold in egg whites. Pour in a greased pan and place in larger pan with hot water. Bake at 325° to 350° 45 min., or until done. Serve warm or cold.

MAPLE PECAN CHIFFON CAKE

2 c. flour	¾ c. wh. sugar	3 tsp. baking pow.
¾ c. br. sugar	¾ c. water	1 tsp. salt
½ c. cooking oil, or salad oil.		½ tsp. cr. of tarter
4 egg yolks, unbeaten		2 tsp. maple flavor
1 c. chopped nuts.		

    Measure sifted flour into sifter, add baking powder and sugar and set aside. In a mixing bowl add the oil, egg yolks, water, maple flavor and nuts, beat well. Then sift in flour mixture. Add brown sugar which has been sifted. Beat 1 min. at low speed. Beat egg, salt and cream of tarter, 5 min. Fold in egg white mixture thoroughly. (This makes a very good cake.) Put in an angel food cake pan.

"Yesterday He loved me, Today, He's just the same; how long will this continue? Forever——Praise His Name!"

POPCORN CAKE

1 c. king syrup (scant)   2 c. sugar
Butter, size of an egg   1½ c. walnut kernels
3 qts. pop corn.

    Melt molasses, sugar and butter, but do not boil. Then add walnuts and popcorn and mix.

RHUBARB CAKE

Cream 1½ c. br. sugar, ½ c. margarine. Add 1 egg. Combine 2 c. flour, ½ tsp. salt, 1 tsp. soda. Add alternately dry ingredients with the above mixture and 1 c. sour milk. Add 1 tsp. vanilla, ½ c. nuts, 2 c. rhubarb (chopped fine). Put in a 9 x 13 pan and sprinkle with ½ c. white sugar and ½ tsp. cinnamon. Bake in a 325° oven for 35 minutes (or until done). Serve with milk and sugar while still warm, or it can be fixed with whipped cream like date pudding.
    —— Mrs. Henry K. Hilty

GRAND CHAMPION SPONGE CAKE

1¼ c. sifted flour   1 c. sugar   ½ tsp. baking pow.
½ tsp. salt   6 egg whites   1 tsp. cr. tartar
½ c. sugar   6 egg yolks   ¼ c. water
1 tsp. vanilla

    Sift together flour, sugar, baking powder and salt. In a mixing bowl, beat egg whites until frothy. Add cream of tartar. Gradually beat in ½ c. sugar a little at a time. Beat until whites form stiff, not dry peaks. In a small bowl combine egg yolks, water, vanilla and sifted dry ingredients. Beat till mixture is light and fluffy. Fold gently into whites. Bake at 350° for 45 min. Frost with Creamy Pineapple Frosting(below).

CREAMY PINEAPPLE FROSTING

    Cream ¼ c. butter and ¼ c. shortening. Gradually add 3 c. sifted confectioners sugar; beat until light and fluffy. Blend in one 8½ oz. can drained, crushed pineapple, 1/8 tsp. salt, 1/4 tsp. vanilla, and ½ tsp. lemon rind. (optional).

SPOTTED CAKE

1 c. lard   3 c. flour   pinch salt.
   Mix this as like pie dough.
2 c. br. sugar   ½ c. cocoa   1 tsp. cinnamon
2 c. sour milk   2 tsp. soda mixed in sour milk
   Gently stir in crumbs to batter and bake at 350°.
— S.S.S.

TEXAS SHEET CAKE

1. Grease cookie sheet. Sift together in large bowl, 2 c. sugar, 2 c. flour, ½ tsp. salt.
2. Bring to a boil 2 bars oleo, 1 c. water, 4 tsp. cocoa.
3. Beat 2 eggs, ½ c. sour milk, 1 tsp. vinegar, 1 tsp. soda.
Add No. 1 and No. 3, then No. 2. Beat well while adding. Bake at 375° for 20 minutes.

ICING

1. Bring to boil 1 bar oleo, 4 tsp. cocoa, 6 tsp. milk.
2. 1 box powdered sugar, 1 tsp. vanilla, 1 c. walnuts.
Add No. 2 to No. 1. Spread on cake as soon as cake is taken from oven.

— Mary Ann Troyer, Apple Creek, Ohio

CHON ADAM'S GIRL

Her hair so strubbly in the wind,
  Her eyes so big and brown,
I often seen her on the road
  When I drove into town.

Chon Adam's girl's grown up, I said.
  And Mom would say—"Yes, well,
The boys'll soon be after her,
  So let her have her spell."

Just like a gawky goldenrod
  She was; and so for play.
She never seen me but she'd yell——
  "Hey, Amos, hey!"

PIES

Pie Crust
(A handwritten addition to her daughter's book)

3 c flour   1 cup lard
1 egg   1 tsp vinegar
1/2 c water   Pinch Salt

In a bowl, add 2.5 cups flour. Cut in 1 cup lard, then add egg, water, vinegar and salt. Continue to add flour a little at a time until dough is the correct consistency to roll out.

ANGEL FOOD PIE

1¼ c. sugar	¼ c. corn starch	¼ tsp. salt
2 c. boiling water	2 egg whites	1 c. crushed pineapple
1 tsp. vanilla		

Sift sugar, corn starch and salt. To this add boiling water and boil until thick. Pour over beaten egg whites and beat well. Add pineapple and vanilla. Pour into baked shell and top with whipped cream.

APPLE BUTTER PIE

½ c. apple butter	2 eggs	½ c. sugar
1½ Tbsp cornstarch	1 tsp. cinnamon	2 c. milk
Pastry for 9" pie.		

Combine first 5 ingredients and mix well, add the milk gradually and blend well. Pour into the unbaked pie shell and cover with lattice top. Bake at 350° for 35 minutes.

APPLE POT PIE

4 large apples	¼ c. shortening	2 c. sifted flour
1/8 tsp. salt	½ to 2/3 c. water	2/3 c. sugar
½ tsp. cinnamon	2 tbsp. butter	2 c. boiling water

Pare apples, core and cut into eighths. Make dough of the shortening, flour and salt, use the water to make a stiff dough. Roll thin like noodle dough. Cout out 2" squares. Arrange alternate layers of apples and dough in a kettle, sprinkling each layer with sugar and cinnamon. Dot the top layer of pastry squares with butter and pour the boiling water in and cover. Cook over low heat for 25-30 minutes or until apples are tender. Serve hot or cold with cream. Serves 6.

APPLE SCHNITZ PIE

1 lb. dried apples	1 qt. cold water	2 Tbsp. cinnamon
1 orange, juice and rind		2 c. sugar
Plain pastry		

Cook schnitz in water to a soft pulp. Add orange juice and rind, cinnamon, salt, sugar and mix well. Cool. Place pie crust in pie pan. Fill with schnitz mixture and cover with top crust. Bake in hot oven 450° 10 minutes and 350° for 30 minutes longer.

APPLE TURNOVERS

Sift together 2 cups flour, ½ tsp. salt, 2 tsp. baking powder and 1/8 tsp. cinnamon. Cut ¾ cup shortening into the mixture. Add just enough milk to moisten. (approx. 5½ tbsp.)

Toss lightly to form a ball of dough, and roll ¼ inch thick into a rectangle. Cut into 6 — 5 inch squares and place 1 peeled sliced apple with 1 tbsp. light brown sugar, a dash of cinnamon, and a dash of nutmeg, dot with butter. Fold corners to make a triangle, pressing edges together with tines of a fork. Arrange on a cookie sheet, ½ inch apart and place in 450° oven. Immediately reduce to 375°. Bake 35-40 min. or until golden brown as pie crust. Can use other fruit or thickened fruit juice. Can also use cherries, blueberries, etc.

——Elizabeth Hilty

BUTTERMILK PIE

3 eggs
1 tsp. vanilla (or rum flavoring)
3 tbsp. (rounded) flour
1 c. buttermilk
1¾ c. sugar
¼ c. melted butter
1 9" pie shell

Beat eggs well, add buttermilk and vanilla. Combine sugar and flour, add to egg mixture. Add melted butter and mix well. Pour into unbaked shell, bake at 350° until set.

BUTTERSCOTCH PIE

1½ c. milk
3 tbsp. flour
1½ c. brown sugar
butter—size of walnut
2 egg yolks

Cook over low heat until thickened. Use egg whites for meringue. Enough for 8½" pie shell.

CARMEL CHIFFON PIE

½ lb. (28) carmels
¼ c. cold water
¾ c. chilled whipped evaporated milk
1 c. hot water
¼ tsp. vanilla
1 pkg. Knox gel.
1 c. chopped nuts
dash of salt

Heat carmels and water till melted. Soften gelatin in ¼ c. cold water. Add to heated mixture. Add salt and vanilla. Chill until slightly thickened. Fold in whipped cream and nuts and pour into a baked pie shell.

——Mrs. Marvin Hilty, Berne, Indiana

CHOCOLATE PIE

1 c. sugar	1 c. Molasses King syrup	1 c. water
½ c. lard	1 tbsp. cinnamon	1 tbsp. cocoa
3 c. flour	pinch of salt	1 tsp. soda

Mix together. Pour in pastry lined pie plates and bake. Frost with chocolate frosting. Makes two 9" pies.

CHOCOLATE PIE

2 c. sugar	1 c. rich milk	1½ tbsp. cocoa
2 egg yolks	2 tbsp. flour	3 c. water
2 tbsp. corn starch	1 tsp. vanilla	

Mix dry ingredients. Add yolk and milk and vanilla. Have water on stove boiling and add to mixture. Bring to a boil and remove. Add 1 tbsp oleo and cool. Pour in pie crust. Makes 2 pies.

CHOCOLATE MOCHA PIE

Soften 1 envelope Knox gelatine in ¼ c. cold water. Combine in sauce pan with 1 tbsp. cocoa, ¾ c. sugar, 1/8 tsp. salt, 1 tsp. instant coffee, 1¼ c. milk.

Bring to a boil, stir constantly. Take from stove. Beat cooked mixture till smooth. Whip 1 cup cream. Add vanilla. Pour into crust. Put nuts on top.

CHOCOLATE ANGEL STRATA PIE

Beat 2 egg whites with: ½ tsp. vinegar, ¼ tsp. salt, and ¼ tsp. cinnamon, until soft mounds form. Add ½ c. sugar, gradually. Continue beating until meringue stands in stiff glossy peaks. Spread in bottom and sides of a baked 9" pie shell. Bake with meringue. Bake at 325° for 15-18 min. till lightly browned. Cool.

CHOCOLATE WHIPPED CREAM FILLING

Add 2 slightly beaten egg yolks and ¼ c. water to 1 c. melted chocolate chips. Mix well. Spread 3 tbsp. over cooled meringue. Chill remainder.

Combine: ¼ c. sugar, ¼ tsp. cinnamon and 1 c. whipping cream. Beat till thick. Spread half of the whipped cream over chocolate in pie shell. Combine remaining whipped cream with the chocolate mixture. Spread over whipped cream in pie shell. Chill at least 4 hours.

COCONUT OATMEAL PIE

3 eggs beaten   2/3 c. white sugar   1 c. br. sugar
2 tsp. oleo (soft)   2/3 c. oatmeal   2/3 c. coconut
2/3 c. milk   1 tsp. vanilla

    Blend together, pour into unbaked pie shell. Bake 30 to 35 minutes.

CORN MEAL PIE

2 eggs beaten   1½ c. br. sugar   3 tbsp. oleo
4 tbsp. cream or Pet milk   2 tbsp. corn meal

    Mix together, put in unbaked pie shell. Bake 300° to 325° for 40 minutes. Add nuts if you like.
    ——Rosie M. Schwartz, Monroe, Ind.

COTTAGE CHEESE PIE

    Prepare a 9 inch pastry shell. Beat 2 eggs until light. Add: ½ c. sugar, beat well. Add 1/8 tsp. salt. ½ c. cream, 2 c. cottage cheese, 2 tbsp. flour, 1 tbsp. lemon juice. Mix well. Pour into pastry shell. Combine 2 tbsp. sugar, ½ tsp. cinnamon and sprinkle over top. Bake in moderate oven 40 minutes, until knife inserted near center comes out clean.   ——M.N.

DONNA'S FRUIT PIE CRUST

5 c. flour   2 c. shortening   1 tbsp. sugar
1 egg, break into cup and fill up with water.
    Mix together, roll out. Real good.

FRUIT PIES

1 qt. black raspberries   1 qt. sour cherries.
    Add sugar and pinch of salt to taste. Add thickening. Put in unbaked pie shell, but crust on top and bake. Makes 3 large pies.

APPLE

    To ½ gal. canned apple snitz, add ½ pt. crushed pineapple, pinch of salt, sugar to taste, and thickening. Makes 3 large 2 crust pies.

PEAR

1 qt. pears sliced   1½ c. pear juice   1 c. sugar
pinch of salt   1 tbsp. cr. pineapple   Unbaked crust.

Boil together and thicken with corn starch. Add black walnut flavor. Put sliced pears in crust, sprinkle crushed soda crackers over pears, add juice and bake.

GRAPENUT PIE

½ c. grapenuts   ¼ c. butter   ½ c. lukewarm water
1/8 tsp. salt,   1 c. br. sugar   3 eggs (beaten)
1 c. dark corn syrup   1 tbsp. vanilla

Soak grapenuts in lukewarm water till water is absorbed. Combine sugar, corn syrup, butter and salt in saucepan. Bring quickly to a boil, stirring until sugar is dissolved, then remove from heat. Beat eggs till foamy. Add small amount of hot syrup at a time to eggs, beating well. Stir in softened grapenuts and vanilla. Pour into unbaked pie shell. Bake at 375° for 40 to 45 minutes. Serve with whipped cream.
——Mrs. Aaron P. Schwartz, Seymour, Missouri

HOBBY PIE or POOR MAN'S PIE

1 unbaked crust   2½ clices of bread, crumbled
½ c. sugar   2 tbsp. flour   Cinnamon to taste
2 c. milk

After piecrust has been place in pie pan, crumble 2½ slices bread into it. In a bowl stir remaining ingredients together. Pour into pie pan. Dot with 1 tbsp. butter. Bake in moderate oven.

LEMON SPONGE PIE

4 tbsp. butter   3½ c. sugar   9 eggs separated
9 tbsp. flour   rind & juice of 3 lemons
pinch of salt.

Mix egg yolks with sugar, flour and salt. Add lemon rind, juice, butter and milk. Fold in stiffly beaten egg whites last. Put in unbaked pie shells. Bake at 425° for 15 minutes then reduce heat to 325° till done. Makes 4 large pies.

LEMON PIE

1 lemon	2 eggs	2 c. sugar
1 c. bread crumbs	2 tbsp. flour	2 c. water
3 c. milk		

Mix together and fill pie crust and put crust on top and bake till done.

MINCE MEAT PIE

Cook 3 quarts ground beef until done, then add 1½ quarts apples, 1 quart apple butter, 5 c. sugar, 1 tbsp. salt, 1 tsp. cinnamon, ¼ tsp. ground cloves, ¼ alspice juice and rind of 2 oranges. Salt to taste. Cook until apples are done.

OH SO GOOD PIE

4 eggs	1½ c. white sugar	2 tbsp. butter
1 tsp. vinegar (scant)	pinch salt	1 c. cooked raisins
1 c. pecans	1 tsp. nutmeg	

Beat egg yolks, add sugar, butter, salt, nutmeg and vinegar. Add raisins and nuts. Beat egg whites until stiff and add to mixture. Bake as usual.

OATMEAL PIE

8 eggs	3 c. green label Karo
3 c. br. sugar	3 c. rolled oats
1 lb. oleo	2 c. coconut and nut meats

Melt oleo, cream sugar, oleo and eggs together. Add Karo and rest of ingredients and mix. Bake in a slow oven Makes 4 pies.

OATMEAL PIE

¼ c. butter	½ c. sugar	½ tsp. cloves
¼ tsp. salt	3 eggs	½ tsp. cinnamon
1 c. dk. corn syrup	1 c. oatmeal	1 unbaked 9" shell

Cream together butter, sugar. Add spice and salt. Stir in syrup. Add eggs and blend well. Stir in rolled oats. Pour into pastry shell. Bake 1 hr at 350° or until knife comes out clean. ——Mrs. John A. Wenger, Chambersburg, Pa.

PECAN PIE

2 eggs beaten pinch of salt ½ c. sugar
1 c. molasses 1 tbsp. flour 1 c. milk
1 tsp. vanilla 2 tbsp. melted butter
1 c. chopped pecans.
    Pour in unbaked pie shell.

PUMPKIN PIE

3 eggs slightly beaten 1 c. sugar ½ tsp. salt
2 tbsp. flour ¼ tsp. cloves ¼ tsp. nutmeg
½ tsp. cinnamon (scant) ¼ tsp. ginger
¾ c. pumpkin 2½ c. rich milk.

    This makes one large pie.

PUMPKIN PIE

2 eggs slightly beaten 1½ c. pumpkin ¾ c. sugar
½ tsp. salt 1 tsp. cinnamon ½ tsp. ginger
¼ tsp. cloves 1 2/3 c. evaporated milk or light cream.
1 9" unbaked pie shell

    Mix filling ingredients in order given. Pour into shell. Bake in preheated hot oven (425°) for 15 minutes. Reduce temperature to moderate (350°) and continue baking for 45 minutes or until knife inserted into center of pie filling comes out clean.
    ——Mrs. Dan R. Yoder, Apple Cree, Ohio

REFRIGERATOR PIE

1 c. milk ½ lb. marshmallows.
    Heat in double boiler till marshmallows are melted. Then add 1 tsp. vanilla, cool until sets. Then beat 1 c. cream and whip into marhmallows. Pour into Graham cracker crust. Put in refrigerator till it sets.

"People are very careful about what they eat, but it is tragic that pure food laws do not apply to what they feed their soul."

RAISIN CUSTARD PIE

2 c. raisins	2 c. water	2 c. sugar
2 tbsp. corn starch	Pinch of salt	2 eggs.

Cook until tender. Add other ingredients and boil. Pour into a baked pie shell.

RAISIN PIE

½ c. raisins	½ c. sugar	1 c. milk
1 heap. tbsp flour	2 eggs	lump butter
1 tsp. vanilla.		

Add enough water to sugar and raisins to cook together well. Mix flour, milk, egg yolks together and add raisins. Boil. Add lump of butter and vanilla. Pour in baked pie shell. Top with egg whites beaten.

RAISIN PIE

1 c. raisins	1 c. sour cream	1 c. sugar
1 egg.		

Mix together, pour into pastry shell and bake.

RHUBARB PIE

2 eggs well beaten	2 tbsp. butter or margarine, melted
3½ c. finely diced rhubarb	1¾ c. sugar
½ tsp. cinnamon ½ tsp. salt	7 tbsp. flour
1 unbaked 9" shell	

Combine eggs, butter and rhubarb. Mix and sift sugar, cinnamon, salt and flour. Add to rhubarb mixture and blend well. Spoon into pastry shell. Bake at 375° for 50 to 60 minutes or until set.

GOOEY SHOO FLY PIE

Syrup		Crumbs
1 c. molasses	½ c. br. sugar	2 c. flour
2 eggs	1 c. hot water	¾ c. br. sugar
1 tsp. soda dissolved in hot water		1/3 c. lard

Put half of syrup in unbaked shell, add half of crumbs on top. Repeat for second pie. Bake 10 min at 400°, then reduce to 350° for 50 minutes.

PENNSYLVANIA SHOO FLY PIE

Juice Part
1 sm. c. br. sugar
1½ lg. c. molasses
2 c. boiling water
2 tsp. soda.
Mix and let cool. Pour in bottom of shell.

Crumb part
3¼ c. flour (large cups)
1 c. brown sugar
½ c. lard
½ tsp. soda
½ tsp. cream tarter
Put on top of juice and

bake 1 hour at 350°.

—Mrs. Sam C. Schwartz, Seymour, Missouri

SHOO FLY PIE

2 unbaked shells   2 c. flour (pastry)
1½ c. br. sugar   4 tbsp. shortening

Mix these ingredients like pie dough for crumbs. Take out 2 c. crumbs for on top of pies. To remainder of crumbs in bowl add: 2 eggs beaten, 2 c. regular molasses or King syrup, 1½ c. hot water. Mix well.

Dissolve 2 tsp. soda in ½ c. hot water. Add to other liquid mixture. Put in pie shells. Put crumbs on top. Bake at 450° for 10 minutes, then at 375° for 30 minutes or till top is dry and done.

SHOO FLY PIE

1 9" pie pan filled with unbaked pastry
¾ c. flour   ½ c. br. sugar   ½ tbsp. butter
½ tbsp. baking soda dissolved in ¾ c. boiling water, then
    slightly cooled.   ½ c. molasses   1 egg yolk beaten

Combine flour and sugar. Cut in butter till crumbly and set mixture aside. Blend egg yolk, molasses and soda-water. Pour this liquid into pie shell and sprinkle reserve crumbs over it. Bake 10 minutes at 450° then reduce to 350° and bake about 20 minutes longer.

SPONGE PIE (CARMEL)

1½ c. br. sugar   2 tbsp. flour   ¼ c. butter
1 c. milk   3 egg yolks   3 egg whites,
    folded in last with 1 tsp. vanilla.
Bake in unbaked crust 40 min or until done (350°)

SUGAR CREAM PIE

1 c. white sugar   2/3 c. br. sugar   ½ c. flour
½ tsp. salt.
   Combine above, then stir in 1 c. boiling water. Add 1 c. light cream, 1/8 tsp. nutmeg, ½ tsp. vanilla. Pour into 9" pastry lined pan. Bake at 450° 10 minutes, then reduce to 350° for 40 minutes.

STRAWBERRY PIE DELUXE

4 c. fresh strawberries, washed and capped
3 tbsp. cornstarch   1 c. sugar   ½ tsp. baking pow.
3 drops red food coloring   1 baked 9" pie shell
   Spread 2 c. whole berries over bottom of pie shell. Mash remaining berries. Add sugar, cornstarch and baking powder and mix well. Place over low heat. Bring to boil, stirring constantly, about 10 minutes. Add food coloring to deepen red of mixture. Cool, then pour over raw berries in pie shell. Refrigerate till thoroughly chilled. Serve with whipped cream.

GRANDMA COBLENTZ'S VANILLA TARTS PIE

First Part
1 c. sugar
1 egg
1 pt. cold water
1 c. molasses
1 tsp. vanilla

Second Part
1 egg
1 c. sugar
3 c. flour
¾ c. sour milk
1 tsp. soda, ½ c. lard
1 tsp. vanilla

   Divide first part in 3 unbaked pie shells. Drop 5 tbsp. of second part in syrup and bake at 375° until done.
      ———Mrs. John Henry Yoder, Virginia Beach, Va.

VANILLA CRUMB PIE

Cook together, 1 c. sugar, 2 c. Karo or molasses, 4 c. water, pinch of salt, 4 tbsp cornstarch, 1 egg well beaten. Then add 1 tsp. vanilla and pour into 3 unbaked pie shells.
   Crumb topping: 2 c. flour, 1 tsp. cr. of tarter, ½ c. lard, 1 tsp. soda, ½ c. sugar. Mix all together until very fine and spread over pudding. Bake until browned.

COOKIES

ANGEL DROPS

2 egg whites
¾ c. sugar
1 tbsp. flour
¼ tsp. salt
½ c. cut up dates
1 tsp. vanilla
1 c. cut up pecans

    Beat eggs, vanilla and salt, add sugar slowly until it forms in peaks. Sprinkle dates and nuts with flour. Fold into egg whites. Drop by teaspoons about 2 inches apart on greased cookie sheet. Bake in $350°$, 10 to 12 minutes. Makes 3 dozen.

BROWN SUGAR COOKIES

4 c. br. sugar
1½ c. sweet milk
4 tsp. vanilla
2 c. lard
4 tsp. soda
2 sifters (8 c.) flour
5 eggs
4 tsp. baking pow.
2 tsp. salt

Mix all above and bake.
                   ———Mrs. Noah M. Beachy

BUTTER BALLS or CHRISTMAS COOKIES

1 c. butter   5 tsp. powdered sugar
Cream together, then add:
1½ c. flour   3 tsp. cold water   1 tsp. vanilla
1 c. chopped nuts.

    Mix all together, make small balls, bake in oven at $350°$ degrees for 10 or 15 minutes. While still hot roll in Powdered sugar, when cold roll in powdered sugar again.

BUTTERMILK COOKIES

2 c. br. sugar   4 or 5 eggs   2 c. wh. sugar
1½ c. lard   2 c. buttermilk (or milk & cream mixed)
4 tsp. baking pow. 4 tsp. soda in a little hot water
salt   4 pts. flour, or nearly 3 qts. more or less.
                  ——Mrs. Elmer Brandenberger

BUTTERSCOTCH COOKIES

6 tbsp. water   4 c. br. sugar   1 c. lard and oleo mixed
4 eggs   7 c. flour   1 tbsp. soda
1 tbsp. cream tartar.

    Cream oleo, lard and sugar, add well beaten eggs and water. Add sifted flour, soda, and cream tartar. Put in rolls, let stand overnight. ——Mrs. E. K. Hilty, Geneva, Ind.

BUTTERMILK COOKIES

2 c. br. sugar
2 eggs
3¾ c. flour
1 c. Crisco
1 c. buttermilk
2 tsp. baking pow.
1 tsp. vanilla
2 tsp. soda

Cream together sugar and crisco, add vanilla and eggs, mix well. Add the soda to the buttermilk, then add to other ingredients. Sift together baking powder and flour., Add this to mixture a little at a time. Mix well. Drop from teaspoon onto ungreased cookie sheet and bake in 350° oven.

FROSTING for BUTTERMILK COOKIES

Melt ¼ c. butter or oleo. Add 1 c. br. sugar, 1 c. milk. Boil together for about 10 min. Let cool slightly. Then add powdered sugar until of spreading consistency. If it gets too stiff before you get done, just add a little milk.
— Mrs. Dan N. Yoder, R. 2, Apple Creek, Ohio

BUTTERSCOTCH DROP COOKIES

⅔ c. butter or oleo
1 tsp. vanilla
2½ c. sifted flour
½ tsp. salt
1½ c. br. sugar
1 tbsp. vinegar
1 tsp. soda
1 c. chopped pecans or California walnuts
2 eggs
1 c. evaporated milk
½ tsp. baking pow.

Cream together butter and brown sugar till light. Add eggs and beat well. Add vanilla and vinegar to evaporated milk. Sift dry ingredients and add alternately with milk to creamed mixture; mix well. Stir in chopped nuts. Drop by rounded tablespoons 2 in. apart, on greased cookie sheet. Bake in moderate oven 350° about 15 minutes, or until firm to touch. Cool, frost with carmel frosting. Top each cookie with pecan or walnut half. These cookies stay soft and keep well.

FROSTING for BUTTERSCOTCH DROP COOKIES

Melt ¼ c. butter or oleo and add 1 cup br. sugar. Boil over low heat 2 minutes, stirring constantly. Add ¼ c. milk and stir till mixture boils up well. Remove from stove and cool until lukewarm, add ¼ tsp. vanilla and 1¾ to 2 c. powdered sugar and beat until smooth.
— Mrs. Lovina Shetler

"Faith makes the uplook good, the outlook bright and the future glorious."

CHOCOLATE COOKIES

3 - 1 oz. sq. unsweetened chocolate	1½ c. sifted flour
1½ tsp. baking pow. ¼ c. butter	½ tsp. salt
1 c. sugar ¾ c. milk	1 egg
1 tsp. vanilla.	

Melt chocolate and butter over hot water; cool; stir in sugar, egg, and vanilla. Sift dry ingredients together; add alternately with milk to creamed mixture, stirring just to blend. Drop by rounded teaspoonfuls onto a greased baking sheet, 2 inches apart. Bake in moderate oven (375°) 8 to 10 minutes. Can be frosted and topped with coconut or chopped nuts. Makes 3½ dozen.

CHOCOLATE CHIP COOKIES

2 c. butter & shortening   2 c. br. sugar
2 c. wh. sugar   4 eggs beaten   2 tsp. soda
2 tsp. hot water   5 c. flour   2 tsp. salt
2 c. chopped nuts   1 12 oz. pkg. chocolate chips
2 tsp. vanilla

Cream shortening and sugars; add beaten eggs. Dissolve soda in hot water, mix alternately with flour sifted with salt. Add nuts and chocolate chips. Flavor with vanilla; drop by teaspoons on greased cookie sheet. Bake 10 to 12 minutes at 375°   —— Mrs. David Y. Schwartz

CHOCOLATE DROPS

2½ c. sugar   ½ c. W. Karo   ½ c. cold water

Boil until it forms a ball in cold water. Beat 2 egg whites. Pour mixture slowly into beaten egg whites while beating. Cool, form in shape, dip in sweet melted chocolate.

CINNAMON BALL COOKIES

1 c. shortening   1½ c. sugar   2 eggs
2¾ c. flour   2 tsp. cr. of tarter   1 tsp. soda
½ tsp. salt

Chill, roll into balls size of a walnut. Roll in a mixture of 2 tbsp. cinnamon and 2 tbsp. sugar. Bake at 400° 8 to 10 minutes. Will puff up at first, then will flatten.

COOKIES

Mix:
1 c. wh. sugar	½ c. br. sugar	¾ c. lard
2 eggs	1 tsp. vanilla	

Add:
2 c. + 2 tbsp flour   1 tsp. soda   ¼ tsp. salt.
Drop by teaspoons on a greased cookie sheet.

CORN MEAL COOKIES

½ c. shortening	½ c. sugar	½ tsp. vanilla
1 egg	1½ c. flour	½ c. corn meal
½ tsp. baking pow.	¼ tsp. salt	½ tsp. nutmeg

Stir or mix as for cookies and roll dough on lightly floured board and cut with 2" cookie cutter. Bake at 400° for about 6 minutes until cookies are very lightly browned. Makes 6 dozen cookies.

CREAM STICKS

½ c. wh. sugar	½ c. lard	2 eggs beaten
3 c. warm water	3 tsp. salt	2 pkg. yeast
¼ c. cool water	8 c. flour.	

Put sugar, lard and salt together. Add 2 c. hot water. Let it dissolve or melt, then add 1 c. cold water, beaten eggs. Soak yeast in lukewarm water. Add to luke warm mixture. Add flour. Let rise once, roll out ½ in. thick, 4 inches long. Fry in hot fat or Mazola corn oil. Keep turning them all the time while frying.

CREAM FILLING

8 c. pow. sugar	¾ tsp. salt	3 egg whites
8 tsp. water	¾ c. white sugar	1 c. Crisco

—MaryAnn Troyer, Apple Creek, O.

DATE DROP COOKIES

1 lb. chopped dates   1 c. boiling water over dates—mash up
1 c. br. sugar   ½ c. wh. sugar   1 tsp. soda
½ c. lard or 1 c. vegetable shortening   3 tsp. baking Pow.
3½ c. flour   1 tsp. cinnamon   1 c. nut meats
1 tsp. vanilla   ¼ tsp. salt.

These stay soft a long time.
—Mrs. Barbara Lambright, Topeka, Ind.

DOUBLE TREAT COOKIES

2 c. sifted flour	2 tsp. baking soda	½ tsp. salt
1 c. shortening	1 c. wh. sugar	1 c. br. sugar packed
2 eggs	1 tsp. vanilla	1 c. peanut butter
1 c. chopped nuts	1 c. chocolate chips	

Mix. Shape in small balls. Place on a cookie sheet. Flatten with a glass dipped in sugar. Bake. They are very crunchy and delicious.

DROP COOKIES

5 eggs	3 c. br. sugar	1 tsp. baking pow.
½ c. oleo or butter	½ c. lard	1 c. cream
1 tbsp (scant) soda		

Flour enough to drop on cookie sheet. Bake 10 minutes at 400°

GINGER COOKIES

¾ c. shortening	1 c. sugar	1 egg
¼ c. dark molasses	2 c. flour	2 tsp. soda
¼ tsp. salt	1 tsp. cinnamon	1 tsp. ginger

Cream shortening and sugar and egg and molasses. Beat well. Add flour and soda, salt and spices. Mix well. Shape into balls about 1½ inches in diameter. Roll in sugar. Place 3 inches apart on cookie sheet. Bake at 350° about 15 minutes.

JUBILEE JUMBO COOKIES

1 c. lard	1 c. wh. sugar	2 tsp. vanilla
2 c. Carnation or top milk		1 tsp. soda
2 c. chopped nuts	2 c. br. sugar	4 eggs
5½ c. sifted flour	2 tsp. salt.	

Mix well shortening, sugar and eggs. Stir in milk, vanilla. Sift together dry ingredients. Blend in the above mixture. Add nuts, chill 1 hour before baking. Bake at 375°, frost while warm. —— Rosie M. Schwartz, Monroe, Ind.

> "No recipe is perfect,
>   Which you may try to fill,
>   Without an ounce of judgment
>   And a like amount of skill."

MIKE LIZZIE COOKIES

Cook 2 lb. raisins in very little water. Cool. Mix together 4 lbs. flour, 2 lbs. wh. sugar, 1 tsp. salt, 1 lb. oleo. Then add the raisins, 5 beaten eggs, 1 pint Brer Rabbit (with orange cap). Mix 3 tbsp. soda and ½ c. boiling water. Add to above mixture. Cool. Lay to rolls on a cookie sheet ½" thick. Brush with beaten egg. Bake. Cool and slice in bars before removing from pans.

MOLASSES COOKIES

2 c. butter or lard   2 c. baking molasses   2 c. sugar
1 c. boiling water   2 tbsp. soda   2 tsp. ginger
2 tsp. salt   little cinnamon

Flour to make a soft dough. Roll ¼ in. thick. Cut and bake in $400°$ oven 10 minutes, or until done.

MOLASSES SUGAR COOKIES

¾ c. shortening,   1 c. sugar   ¼ c. Brer Rabbit Molasses
2 tsp. soda   1 egg   2 c. sifted all purpose flour
1 tsp. cinnamon   ½ tsp. salt

Melt shortening in a 3 or 4 qt. saucepan over low heat. Remove from heat; let cool. Add sugar, molasses and egg; beat well. Sift flour, soda, cinnamon and salt; add to first mixture. Mix well; chill. Form in 1 inch balls, roll in granulated sugar and place on greased cookie sheets two inches apart. Bake at $375°$ for 8 to 10 minutes.

——Mrs. Sam Y. Schwartz

MOLASSES COOKIES

¾ c. shortening   1 tsp. cinnamon   2 tsp. soda
1 c. sugar   ½ tsp. salt   ¼ c. molasses
1 egg   ½ tsp. cloves   ½ tsp. ginger
2 c. sifted flour

Cream shortening and sugar; stir in molasses and egg. Sift dry ingredients together; stir into molasses mixture. Beat well. Form in 1 inch balls. Place 2 inches apart on ungreased cookie sheet; bake in moderate oven ($375°$) about 12 minutes. Makes about 3 dozen.

"One man with a glowing experience of God is worth a library full of arguments!"

MYSTERY BARS

½ c. margarine   ½ c. br. sugar   1 c. sifted flour
   Mix 2 min. Bake at 325° 20 minutes
Second: 2 eggs,   1/8 tsp. salt   1 tsp. vanilla
2 tbsp. flour   ½ tsp. Baking powder.
   Beat 2 minutes. Add nuts. Beat enough to blend. Spread over partly baked dough. Bake at 325° for 25 minutes. Cut while warm. Makes 2 dozen.

NO BAKE COOKIES

¾ c. oleo   2 c. sugar   6 oz. evaporated milk
   Combine and bring to a rolling boil and add 1 pkg. instant pudding and stir then. Add 3 cups quick rolled oats. STir until thick enough to put by spoonfuls on wax paper.

GAYS ICE BOX OATMEAL COOKIES

1 c. lard   1 c. wh. sugar   1 c. br. sugar packed
Cream together. Then add 2 beaten eggs and 1 tsp. vanilla.
Sift together: 1½ c. flour   1 tsp. soda
   1 tsp. salt.
Then mix all together. Add 3 c. oatmeal, ½ c. shredded coconut. Mix well. Then put in roll and chill.
   ——Mrs. Elmer K. Hilty, Geneva, Ind.

GUMDROP OATMEAL COOKIES

1 c. butter   1 c. brown sugar   1 c. wh. sugar
2 eggs   1 tsp. vanilla   2 c. sifted flour
1 tsp. soda   1 tsp. baking pow.   ¼ tsp. salt
2 c. quick oats   1 c. flaked coconut   1 c. chopped walnuts
1 c. colored gumdrops, cut up.
   Cream butter and sugars together; add eggs and vanilla; beat well. Sift dry ingredients together; stir into creamed mixture. Add remaining ingredients. Drop by spoonfuls on ungreased baking sheet, 2 inches apart. Bake in moderate oven (375°) for 10 minutes.

   "Envy is a spiritual poison that always proves fatal to love."

WALNUT OATMEAL CRISPS

1 c. shortening	1½ c. flour	1 c. br. sugar
1 tsp. salt	1 c. wh. sugar	1 tsp. soda
2 beaten eggs	3 c. oatmeal	1 tsp. vanilla
½ c. chopped nuts		

Cream shortening and sugar; add eggs and vanilla; beat well. Add sifted dry ingredients, oats and nuts. Form long rolls and chill. Slice ¼ in. thick. Bake at 350° for 10 min.

OATMEAL COOKIES

2 c. br. sugar	¾ tsp. salt	1 c. lard
2 c. flour (scant)	1 egg	1 tsp. vanilla
1 tsp. soda	1½ c. quick oatmeal	
2 tsp. baking pow.	Nut meats.	

Roll in balls size of a walnut, bake 8 to 10 min at 350°
——Mrs. Sam Schwartz, Mrs. Leah Schwartz, Mrs. Peter E. A. Schwartz, Seymour, Mo.

OATMEAL COOKIES

1 c. br. sugar	1 c. wh. sugar	2 c. oatmeal
1 c. cooked raisins	1 c. lard — pour hot over above	
1 tsp. cinnamon	1 tsp. cloves	1 tsp. soda
½ c. hot water	3 eggs	1 tbsp. sweet milk
3 c. flour	2 tsp. baking pow.	½ c. nuts.

Drop by teaspoons on cookie sheet.

RAISIN OATMEAL BARS (real good)

1 c. raisins	¼ c. hot water	1¼ c. br. sugar
1/3 c. shortening	2 eggs (unbeaten)	1 tsp. vanilla
1 c. flour	½ tsp. salt	1 tsp. baking pow.
½ c. rolled oats	½ c. chopped nuts.	

Combine raisins and hot water; set aside. Beat together sugar, shortening, eggs and vanilla until smooth and creamy. Stir in flour sifted with salt and baking powder. Blend in raisin-water mixture. Then oats and nuts. Spread evenly in greased 13" x 9" baking pans. Bake at 375° for 20 to 22 minutes, or until done when tested. Cool in pan. Cut into bars or squares and roll in powdered sugar.

ORANGE COOKIES

Cream 2 c. br. sugar and 1 c. shortening well together, add 2 eggs, beat well, add 1 orange (put through food grinder). Add: 1 c. sour cream, ½ tsp. salt, 1 tsp. soda dissolved in cream. Sift 2 tsp. baking powder with 5 c. flour, (I usually don't use quite 5 cups so they aren't so dry.) Bake for 15 to 18 minutes in 400° oven.

FROSTING: 1 orange rind ground fine, 2 tbsp. butter add powdered sugar till thick enough to spread. Frost while warm.

PEANUT BUTTER COOKIES

3¼ c. flour, 2 tsp. soda 1 tsp. salt
1 c. sugar 1 c. br. sugar packed
2 eggs 1 c. shortening (½ oleo)
1 c. peanut butter 4 tbsp. milk 2 tsp. vanilla
1 pkg. candy kisses

Cream sugars and shortening, add eggs, peanut butter, vanilla, milk. Stir until well mixed. Add dry ingredients mixture. Shape into balls, using a rounded teaspoon for each. Roll ball in sugar, press a bit with a fork or put candy kisses on top and press down firmly until cookie cracks. Bake 10 to 12 minutes at 375°. ——Mrs. Dave Y. S.

DELICIOUS PEANUT BUTTER COOKIES

1 c. shortening 1½ c. wh. sugar 1 c. peanut butter
2 eggs 1 tsp. vanilla ½ tsp. salt
½ tsp. soda 2½ c. flour

Drop by teaspoons on cookie sheet. Bake at 370° for 12 minutes. Makes about 50 cookies.
——Mrs. Petie E. A. Schwartz, Seymour, Mo.

PEANUT BUTTER BARS

1 1/3 c. shortening 2 c. peanut butter 1 c. br. sugar
3 c. wh. sugar 1 tsp. salt 8 eggs.
1½ tsp. vanilla Mix all these together.

Then add 4 c. sifted flour, and 4 tsp. baking powder. Mix well, then add 1 c. (packed) coconut. and mix. Spread ½ thick on greased baking sheet. Bake at 350° for 20 mins. Cool. Cut into bars. —— Mary Ann Troyer, Apple Creek, Ohio

PEANUT WHIRL COOKIES

½ c. shortening 1¼ c. sifted flour 1 c. sugar
½ c. peanut butter ½ tsp. salt ½ tsp. soda
1 egg 1 tsp. vanilla 2 tbsp. milk
1 pkg. (6 oz.) chocolate bits

Cream shortening, sugar, peanut butter, egg and vanilla. Add sifted dry ingredients with milk. Roll out cookie dough to rectangle shape ¼ inch thick. Melt choc. bits over hot water and spread on cookie dough. Roll jelly roll fashion and chill ½ hour. Slice with a sharp knife into thin slices (1/8 inch) and bake at 350° 8 to 10 minuges. Yields 5 to 6 dozen.

FILLED RAISIN COOKIES

Dough Filling
2 c. sugar 1 c. milk 2 c. chopped raisins
4 tsp. cr. tarter 1 c. shortening 2 tbsp. flour
7 c. flour 2 tsp. soda 1 c. water
2 tsp. baking pow. 2 eggs 1 c. sugar
2 tsp. vanilla (boil till thick)

Mix and roll thin. Use a thimble to make little holes in cookie for filling.

SHINGLE COOKIES

3 c. br. sugar 1 c. hot water 1 c. shortening
1 tsp. baking pow. Flavor to taste

Add raisins or nuts if desired. Add enough flour to make dough like a thick cake dough. Spread in pan, bake and cut while warm. Can be iced. Bake at 400° for 10 minutes.

SOFT SUGAR DROP COOKIES

1½ lb. lard 3 lb. br. sugar 6 eggs beaten
1 qt. thick milk, or buttermilk 2 tbsp. soda in milk
3¾ lb. flour vanilla to taste.

Bake in hot oven at 450°. Dust with powdered sugar if desired. — —Elsie Peachy, Mifflintown, Pa.

"O weary Moms mixing dough
 Don't you wish that food would grow?
Your lips would smile, I know, to see,
 A cookie bush or a donut tree."

WHOOPIE PIES

2 c. white sugar
4 c. flour
pinch of salt
1 c. sour milk.

2 eggs
1 c. hot water
2 tsp. vanilla

1 c. shortening
2 tsp. soda
1 c. cocoa

Sift dry ingredients, cream eggs, sugar and shortening. Add sour milk. (add 2 tbsp vinegar to sweet milk to sour it.) Mix alternately then add hot water last. Drop on cookie sheet and bake about 8 min. or until done.

––Mrs. Amos Yoder, Kenton, Ohio
––Mrs. John Hilty, Bryant, Ind.
––Mrs. Daniel C. Schwartz, Geneva, Ind.

A RECIPE TO LIVE BY

Blend one cup of love and one half cup of kindness, add alternately in small portions one cup of appreciation and three cups of pleasant companionship into which has been sifted three teaspoons of deserving praise.

Flavor with one teaspoon carefully chosen advice. Lightly fold in one cup of cheerfulness to which has been added a pinch of sorrow.

Pour with tender care into small clean hearts and let bake until well matured. Turn out on the surface of society, humbly invoke God's blessing and it will serve all mankind.

DESSERTS
Puddings
Ice-cream

APPLE CRISP

½ c. butter   1 c. flour   1 c. br. sugar
4—6 medium sized apples   2 tsp. cinnamon

Slice apples in casserole. Serve with crumbs made from the ingredients and bake ¾ hour at 350°.

APPLE CRUNCH

Place in a baking dish, 4 cups apples, ½ c. sugar, 1 tbsp. flour. Sprinkle with nutmeg. Top with the following: ¾ c. oatmeal (quick), ¼ c. sifted flour, ¼ c. br. sugar, ¼ c. wh. sugar, ¼ c. butter. Mix. Bake at 375° until apples are done.
——Mrs. Amos Yoder, Kenton, Ohio

BROKEN GLASS

Dissolve 1 red, 1 green, 1 orange box of jello separately in 1½ c. of hot water for each box and pour each in a square pan. When jello is ready, dissolve 2 envelopes of plain gelatin in 1½ c. cold water.

Bring to a boil 1 c. pineapple juice and 3 tbsp. sugar. Add the softened gelatin and cold water to this and stir well. Whip 1 pt. cream and fold in the gelatin mixture, also the jello all cut in cubes. Pour into a pan lined with 24 graham crackers rolled into crumbs, and ½ c. sugar and ¼ c. butter added. Bake this crust at 250° for 15 minutes and chill before pour-in the gelatin and cream mixture. Sprinkle a few crumbs on top. Chill at least 3 hrs. It is easily made a day before serving and since it makes a big batch, it is nice for group serving.
——Mrs. Melvin Kuhno, Ligonier, Ind.

CHRISTENA'S PUDDING

2/3 c. flour   2 rounded tbsp. cocoa   ½ tsp. salt
¾ c. sugar   4 c. milk   1 tsp. vanilla

For vanilla pudding add 2 eggs and omit cocoa.
——Mrs. Sarah Brandenberger

CARAMEL TAPIOCA PUDDING

7 c. boiling water   ½ tsp. salt   1½ c. baby pearl tapioca
    Boil this till clean, then add
4 egg yolks   ½ pt. cream.
    Let come to boil, then take off fire. Beat eggs in, cream well together, then add:
3 c. br. sugar   1 stick butter or margarine
¼ tsp. soda   1/3 c. hot water.
    Boil this while you are making the above, it is a caramel. Then pour to above and stir good, let cool. Then when I am ready to serve, I add 1 pkg. Lucky Whip, whipped and cut in. Add bananas and 1 Baby Ruth bar if you want to.
    —— Barbara Lambright, Topeka, Ind.

CHOCOLATE BAR DESSERT

20 large marshmallows   1 c. whipping cream
½ c. milk   1½ c. graham crackers crumbs
6 almond candy bars   6 tbsp. oleo melted

In a small sauce pan combine marshmallows and milk, stir over med. heat till marshmallows are melted. Remove from heat, break chocolate bars into pieces. Add to marshmallow mixture, stirring until bars are melted. Cool till partially set. Whip cream; fold into chocolate mixture. Blend graham cracker crumbs and melted butter. Pat ¾ cup of the crumbs in bottom of 8 x 8 x 2 inch baking pan. Pour chocolate mixture over. Cover with remaining crumbs. Chill 3 or 4 hours.
    —— Mrs. David R. Wickey, New Haven, Ind.

CHOCOLATE ICE BOX PUDDING

1 lg. (10¾ oz) Sweet Milk Chocolate Bar
2 tbsp. hot water. (put in chocolate while melting)
3 tbsp. sugar   4 eggs separated   1 tsp. vanilla
½ c. chopped nuts   1 c. whipping cream 1 pkg. van. wafers

Melt chocolate over hot water. Add the 2 tbsp. water to chocolate while melting, add egg yolks and sugar. Cool. Add nuts and vanilla. Beat egg whites, also cream, fold together. Then fold in choc. mixture. Line bottom of bowl with wafers, then choc. mixture. Cream & nuts on top.

DAIRY QUEEN

Soak: 2 env. Knox gelatine in ½ c. cold water.
Heat: 4 c. whole milk until hot but not boiling
     Remove from heat.
Add: Gelatin   2 tsp. vanila
                 2 c. sugar   3 c. cream
Put in ice box to chill 5 or 6 hrs. before freezing. Makes 1 gallon. Ingredients may be varied to suit taste.
                  ——Mrs. Crist K. Hilty, Berne, Ind.

DATE PUDDING

1 c. sugar   2/3 c. milk   1 tbsp. butter
2 tsp. baking pow 1 c. dates
    Drop dough in boiling syrup made with:
2 c. br. sugar   ½ c. butter   2 c. boiling water
    Bake 20 min in moderate oven (350°) Serve with whipped cream.   ——Mrs. John K. Hilty

FROZEN CUSTARD

Heat 2 qts. milk. Soak 4 level tbsp. gelatin in ½ c. water for 5 minutes.
    4 c. wh. sugar   1¼ tsp. salt.
Put the above together and cool until set. Add 1 qt. cream, 1 qt. milk and 3 tbsp. vanilla. This fills a gallon and a half freezer.   ——Anna Beachy

FRUIT CHEESE CAKE (A PUDDING)

Mix 16 graham crackers, crushed, ¾ c. gran. sugar, ½ stick butter or oleo. Press in 9 x 13 cake pan. Mix 2 eggs, beaten, 1 cup gran. sugar, 2 - 8 oz. pkgs cream cheese, 1 tsp. vanilla. Spread over graham crackers. Bake 15 minutes at 375°. When cool pour any fruit pie filling over it. Then chill. Serve with whipped cream on top.

GRAPE NUT PUDDING

½ c. butter   2 c. sugar   4 egg yolks
4 tbsp. flour   ½ c. Grape nuts 2 c. milk
4 egg whites beaten stiff   Juice and rind of 1 lemon
    Set in pan of hot water in oven 40-50 minutes at 350°

HOLIDAY RIBBON SALAD

1 box lime jello   1 c. crush. pineapple   1½ c. water or juice
    Put in bottom of pan let get firm.
1 box lemon jello,   3 oz. Phil. cr. cheese   1 c. scant milk
    Whip cheese in 1 c. hot water and jello.
    Put on top of lime jello and let set again till firm.
1 box. cherry jello   1¾ c. water or juice   2 apples
1 orange (grind with peelings)   Nuts if desired.
    Put on top of it and serve with whipped cream.
                ——Miss Lucinda Hilty, Monroe, Ind.

ORANGE DESSERT

2 - 3 oz. pkg. orange gelatin   1 c. boiling water
1 pt. orange sherbert   1 - 11 oz. can mandarin oranges
1 c. heavy cream whipped.
    Dissolve gelatin in boiling water. Add sherbet and mix well, when partially set, (it sets swiftly) add oranges and fold in whipped cream, chill.
              ——Mrs. N. N. Miller, Topeka, Ind.

PEACH CRUNCH

Place 1 qt. peaches in baking dish. Mix 1 tbsp. flour and peach juice, and 1 tbsp. sugar and pour over peaches. Combine 1 c. sugar, 1 c. flour, 2 tsp. baking powder, ½ tsp. salt, 2 tbsp. butter and 1 egg. Sprinkle over top of peach mixture. Bake at 400° degrees. Serve with milk.
              ——Mrs. Amos Yoder, Kenton, Ohio

PINEAPPLE DESSERT

1st Part: 2 boxes lemon jello, dissolve with 2 c. hot water. Add 2 c. cold water. Add 1 can crushed pineapple, drained. Mix well, and pour in a square cake pan and chill.

2nd Part: 2 env. Dream Whip. 8 oz. pkg. cream cheese. Whip the Dream Whip according to pkg. directions, add cream cheese and cream well. Pour over 1st part.

3rd Part: Squeeze juice out of pineapples. Add water to make 2 cups. Add 1 c. sugar, 3 tbsp. flour, pinch salt, 3 egg yolks. Beat with egg beater and heat till it thickens. Cool and pour over 2nd part.

CANDY
Frostings

Pop Corn Balls

1 c Sugar
1 c Half & Half
1 c White Syrup
6 qts. Popped Popcorn

Cook to Soft Ball Stage. (235-240°) Test a little drop in cup of cold water. Pick it up. If the syrup holds its shape when formed into a ball underwater but loses its shape when removed, it is ready. Beat a couple of minutes, then pour over the popped popcorn.

Pumpkin Bars

2 c Sugar
1 c oil
4 eggs
2 c flour
2 c pumpkin
2 tsp baking powder
1 tsp vanilla
1 tsp cinnamon
1 tsp baking soda
¼ tsp salt

Preheat oven to 350°. Mix all ingredients together. Pour into a greased 10x15 shallow pan. Bake 20-25 minutes and allow to cool the frost with cream cheese icing below.

Cream Cheese Icing

1 sm pck cream cheese
1 tsp vanilla
2 T milk
¾ stick oleo
3 c powdered sugar

Blend all ingredients with mixer until creamy. Spread on top of bars.

BEST CARAMEL FROSTING

1 c. br. sugar packed   ½ c. butter   ¼ c. milk
1¾ to 2 c. sifted confectioners sugar.

    Melt butter, add brown sugar and cook over low heat for 2 minutes, stirring constantly. Add milk and continue stirring until mixture comes to a boil. Remove from heat and cool. Add confectioner's sugar until of right consistency to spread.   ——Mrs. Esther Miller, LaGrange, Ind.

BUTTER CREAM FROSTING

1 lb. powdered sugar   ½ c. soft butter or oleo
1/3 tsp. salt   1 tsp. vanilla   3 or 4 tbsp. milk

CAKE ICING

10 tbsp. br. sugar   6 tbsp. melted butter   1 tsp. vanila
½ c. coconut   5 tbsp. cream

    Spread on cake and return to oven until it bubbles.
        ——Mrs. Howard Miller

CANDIED GRAPEFRUIT PEEL

4 grapefruit   4 c. sugar   ¼ tsp. salt
3½ c. water   1 tbsp. plain gelatine.

    Peel grapefruit and cut peelings in ¼ in. strips. Place in large pan, cover with water. Bring to boil and boil 15 to 20 minutes. Drain. Repeat twice with fresh water each time. Drain. Return peel to pan and add sugar, water and salt, cook over low heat, stirring occasionally, one to two hours or til syrup is thick and peel clear. Remove from heat, add gelatine, stir until dissolved. Let peel stand in syrup till cold. Drain. Roll pieces in sugar. Place on cake rack to try 24 to 48 hours. STore in covered container in cool place. Makes 2½ lbs. You can also do orange or lemon peel the same way. And use it in baking or eat like candy.

CHOCOLATE DROPS

1 c. cream   2 c. wh. sugar   Boil 10 munutes
Add ¼ tsp. cr. tarter —— boil a little longer.
Then set in cool place, let stand till luke warm. Beat till it can be formed in drops. Dip in chocolate.

CARMEL CORN

7 c. popped corn   1 c. sugar   1/3 c. water
1/3 c. corn syrup   1 tsp. salt   ¼ c. oleo
1 tsp. vanilla.   (cook to 250 degrees)
     Remove from heat, stir in vanilla and pour over corn.

CARAMEL ICING

1 c. br. sugar   3 tbsp. Crisco   2 tbsp. butter
pinch of salt.
     Bring to a boil and add ¼ c. milk. Boil slowly for 3 minutes. Take off and cool, then sift 1½ c. powdered sugar and beat well. Add vanilla.
     ——Howard Esther Miller, Lagrange, Ind.

CARAMEL ICING

2 c. br. sugar   2 tbsp. butter   ½ c. cream
     Cook over low heat, for 5 minutes, then cool. Add powdered sugar and Crisco as much as desired.

CARAMEL NUT SLICES

1 c. shortening (soft and part butter)   2 c. br. sugar
2 eggs   3½ c. flour, sifted   1 tsp. soda
½ tsp. salt   1 c. finely chopped nuts.
     Cream shortening, sugar and eggs. Sift together dry ingredients, mix and add nuts. Shape in 2 rolls 2 inches across, chill, slice and bake 8 to 10 min. in 400° oven.

CHOCOLATE FROSTING

Combine 2 c. of confectioners sugar, 3 tbsp. cocoa, pinch of salt. Sift into medium sized bowl. Blend 2 or 3 rounded tbsp. butter or shortening and ½ tsp. vanilla. Gradually add 4 to 5 tbsp. boiling water while mixing to a spreading consistancy. Cocoa may be omitted and other color or flavor added.
     ——Mrs. Howard (Esther) Miller

"Live each short hour with God, and the long years will take care of themselves."

CHOCOLATE FUDGE

32 marshmallows, melted ¼ c. water 2 1/3 c. wh. sugar
¼ lb. margarine   6 oz. evaporated milk ¼ tsp. salt
1½ c. chocolate chips

    Bring to a boil, cook for exactly 8 minutes. Remove from heat, stir in marshmallows, then add chocolate chips, stir until dissolved. Add 1 cup pecans.
    ——Sevilla Yoder, Virginia Beach, Va.

CHRISTMAS CARAMEL CANDY

4 c. br. sugar   2 c. white Karo   3 pts. cream

Mix 1 pt. cream with the Karo and sugar. Boil to soft ball and add another pint of cream and boil to soft ball again. Then add the 3rd pint of cream and boil to soft ball again. Add a piece of paraffin the size of a walnut. Add 2 c. nuts if desired and 1 tbsp. vanilla. Pour in greased pans. When cool, cut in pieces and wrap in wax paper. Very good! (This has to be stirred all the time while it's cooking)

CORN FLAKE CLUSTERS

½ c. corn syrup   3 tbsp. sugar   3 tbsp. oleo or butter
2 c. corn flakes   ½ c. flaked coconut ½ c. chopped nuts

    Combine corn syrup, sugar and margarine in medium size sauce pan. Bring to boil over medium heat, stirring constantly. Continue boiling 5 minutes while stirring. Remove from heat. Add remaining ingredients mixing thoroughly. Drop by level tablespoons full onto waxed or buttered baking sheets. Cool until firm. Yield: about 24.
    ——Mrs. Joe B. Byler, N.W., Pa.

CRACKER JACK

12 c. popped corn
Boil to a hard ball the following: 1 c. br. sugar
½ c. karo and molasses 1 tsp. vinegar ½ c. water
2 tsp. butter.

    Stir in ¼ tsp. soda. Mix and pour over pop corn. Bake in slow oven ½ hour——keep stirring. Store in something tight.   ——E. K. F., Arizona

CREAM CHEESE ICING

Blend together 1 box or 2 c. of sifted powdered sugar, 1 stick of butter and one 8 oz. cream cheese and vanilla.

CREAMY QUICK FUDGE

1 c. choc. chips   1 tsp. vanilla   1 c. pow. sugar
¼ tsp. salt   ½ stick soft butter or margarine
6 tbsp. evap. milk at room temperature   1 c. pecans or
      walnut pieces. Melt chocolate pieces over hot (not boiling) water. Combine in mixing bowl powdered sugar, evaporated milk, vanilla and salt; stir until smooth. Add melted chocolate; stir until blended. Stir in soft butter. Mix in nuts. Spread in buttered 8" square pan; chill until firm, then cut into squares. Makes about 1½ lbs. candy.

CRUNCHY FUDGE SANDWICHES

     Melt one 6 oz. pkg (1 c.) Nestle's butter scotch morsels with ½ c. peanut butter in heavy saucepan over low heat, stirring till blended. Stir in 4 c. Rice Krispies cereal. Press half of mixture into buttered 8" square pan. Chill. Set remainder aside.

     Stir over hot water one 6 oz. pkg. (1 c.) chocolate chips, ½ c. sifted confectioners sugar, 2 tablespoons butter, 1 tbsp. water, till chocolate melts. Spread over chilled mixture. Top with reserved misture. Chill. Cut into 1½" squares. Yield: 25 squares.

FROSTING

2 c. coconut   1/3 c. cream   2 tsp. vanilla
1 1/3 c. br. sugar   8 tbsp. butter

     Mix together and spread over warm cake. Put in oven again and brown 3 to 5 minutes.

FROSTING

1 stick oleo   1/3 c. buttermilk   1 heap. tbsp. cocoa
     Mix and bring to a boil. Then add 1 box powdered sugar and 1/3 c. nuts, 1 tsp. vanilla. Spread frosting on hot cake just as it comes from the oven.   —— M. S.

"Christians who move the world, do not let the world move them."

GOOD FROSTING

1½ c. sugar   ¼ c. butter   1 c. milk
1 c. pecans.

Mix sugar, milk and butter. Boil 3 to 5 minutes. Beat until thickened. Pour on cake while hot, add nuts.

HERSHEY BAR CANDY

Mix 4½ c. sugar, ¼ lb. butter or oleo and 1 can Carnation milk and boil 7½ minutes, remove and add 1 pkg. chocolate chips and 16 candy bars. Stir until dissolved, pour in pans. Have them broken up and ready when taken from stove as it will not take long to get thick. (This is really a good fudge and it is always taken before other candy.)

MARSHMALLOW TREATS

¼ c. oleo or butter   10 oz. pkg. marshmallows (40)
5 c. Rice Krispies cereal   (or 4 c. miniature marshmallows)

Melt margarine in 3 quart saucepan. Add marshmallows and cook over low heat, stirring constantly, until marshmallows are melted and mixture is very syrupy. Remove from heat.

Then add Rice Krispies and stir until well coated. Press warm mixture evenly and firmly into buttered 13 x 9 x 2 inch pan. Cut into squares when cool. Yield: 24. (Note: about 2 cups marshmallow creme may be substituted for marshmallows. Add to melted margarine and cook over low heat for about 5 minutes, stirring constantly. Proceed as directed in second step above.)

OH HENRY BARS

3 c. wh. sugar   ½ c. Karo   1 c. water
¾ c. peanut butter.

Boil until above forms a soft ball, then add 3/4 c. peanut butter. Stir until it thickens, shape and let cool. Then cook 1 c. Karo and ½ c. water and ½ c. br. sugar. Dip balls into this syrup then roll in broken peanuts while it is hot. Coat with melted chocolate.

FUDGE
(added later in Author's original cookbook)

3 c. choc. chips   1 cn Sweetened Cond. Milk
½ stick butter

Microwave 2 minutes, stir, microwave 2 min, pour in pan

MILKY WAY BARS

Part 1. 3 c. wh. sugar 1½ c. Karo
1 c. water. Cook this to hard ball stage, then remove from fire. Quickly beat up stiff, whites of 3 eggs and slowly add the syrup, stirring constantly until it becomes stiff. Add flavoring and beat 1 tbsp. cocoa in whites of eggs. Pour in pan.

Part 2. Carmel Candy 1 lb. br. sugar
½ lb. butter 1 tsp. cr. tarter 1 c. wh. Karo
1 can Eagle Brand milk. Boil this together 12 minutes, stirring all the time. Add nuts (1 c.). Pour on top of part 1. (It don't take it all for one batch, just use as much as you wish.) Now put where cold till hard. Cut in small oblong bars and dip in melted chocolate. Just work with a few pieces at a time, keep rest where cold.

MINTS

1 lb. pow. sugar 4 tbsp. oleo melted 1 lg. egg white
4 drops coloring 9 drops oil flavoring (must be oil to hold flavor)

Use glass eyedropper to be accurate. A plastic one is eaten by oil. Add the color with the melted oleo. Vary the mints by adding chocolate, nuts, peanut butter, etc. Kneead the ingredients until you get the right consistency. Keep the ball wrapped in wax paper or plastic, while making the mints to prevent drying. If you freeze the mints that makes the texture creamy. You can freeze them immediately or the next day. Should be frozen at least 24 hours before eating. Store in air tight containers, wrapped in wax paper or plastic, do not use foil. Do not freeze more than 6 weeks.

PRALINES

2 c. wh. sugar 1 tsp. soda 1 c. buttermilk
pinch of salt.

Put all in 8 qt. kettle, stir a little. Cook briskly, stirring frequently, scraping bottom and corners for about 5 minutes. Now add 2 tbsp. butter and 2 c. pecans. Stir continuously for about 5 minutes, or till it forms very soft ball in cold water. Remove from heat, let stand for a minute or two, now beat till thick and creamy. Immediately drop by teaspoons on wax paper.

BREADS
ROLLS
Pancakes

BREAD

3 c. warm water   1 pkg. yeast   3 tbsp. sugar
1 tbsp salt   3 tbsp. lard

Add enough flour to make a soft dough. Bake at 425° for 30 minutes or until done.
——Mrs. Howard Miller

BROWN BREAD

½ c. br. sugar   1 c. flour   2 c. graham flour
1 tsp. soda   1 tsp. salt   2 c. buttermilk
1 c. raisins   ½ c. molasses

Combine dry ingredients in large bowl; add buttermilk, raisins and molasses. Mix well. Grease four pans well; divide dough into pans. Do not fill over ¾ full. Let rise for 1 hour. Bake at 350° for 1 hour. Remove from pans 5 minutes after removing from oven. Good served hot or cold.
——Mrs. M. N. E., Bryant, Ind.

DILLY CASSEROLE BREAD

1 pkg. yeast   1 tbsp. sugar   ¼ c. warm water
1 tbsp. butter   1 c. cott. cheese   1 tsp. salt
¼ tsp. soda   1 egg   2¼–2½ c. flour
1 tsp. dill seed   1 tbsp. minced onion

Soften yeast in water. Combine cheese, sugar, onion, butter, dill, salt, soda, egg and softened yeast. Add half of the flour and beat with electric mixer. Then knead in rest of flour. Form into loaf in bread pan and let rise. Bake at 350° about 40 minutes or until done. Very good.
——Mrs. Liechty

HOME MADE BREAD

6 c. lukewarm water   6 tsp. salt   6 tbsp. sugar
3 pkg. yeast   9 tbsp. melted shortening
Enough flour to make soft dough

Let rise till double in size. Work down. Let rise again. Work down and form loaves and put in pans. Let rise again. Bake in 350° to 375° oven for about ½ hour.
———Mrs. E. D. Schwartz, Berne, Indiana

"Before you begin to give some one a piece of your mind, consider carefully whether you can spare any."

HOME MADE BREAD

2½ soup spoons yeast   ½ c. lard   5 c. water
5 tbsp. sugar   2½ tbsp. salt

Add flour till it makes elastic dough. Let rise 20 min. Knead good. Let rise 20 minutes. Put in pans. Makes about 4 loaves   —— M.J.H., Berne, Ind.

WHOLE WHEAT BREAD

Melt 1 stick margarine. Add 2 2/3 c. milk and heat to scalding. Cool to lukewarm. Dissolve 1 cake Fleischman's yeast in 2 c. warm water. 2 beaten eggs. 1 heaping c. sugar, 2 tsp. salt. Mix all ingredients and add 5 c. whole wheat flour, and 7 to 8 c. white flour or enough to finish. Finish as with white bread. Makes 4 loaves.

CINNAMON FLUFF

1 c. sugar   1 tbsp. oleo   1 c. milk
2½ c. flour   2½ tsp. baking pow. Pinch of salt.

Cream sugar and oleo. Then add other ingredients. Dot with oleo and sprinkle brown sugar and cinnamon. Bake. This is best when served warm.

CORN BREAD

1 c. corn meal   ½ tsp. salt   1 or 2 eggs
1 c. whole wheat flour   1 c. milk
¼ c. sugar   4 tsp. baking pow. ¼ c. shortening
                                                       (melted or lard)

Sift together dry ingredients. Add milk, well beaten eggs and shortening. Bake in greased pan 20 to 25 minutes at 400° degrees. ——Mrs. Howard (Esther) Miller

"Don't worry about wringing the water out of your budget. The financial squeeze will take care of that"

"Persons with whom you have mutual interests are usually those whom you can bank on for lasting friendship"

"A good way to make people suspicious of you is to smile a lot."

CINNAMON ROLLS

2 cakes yeast	½ c. sugar	¼ c. lukewarm water
1 tsp. salt	1 c. scalded milk	2 eggs, well beaten
¼ c. butter	5 c. flour	

Put yeast to dissolve in ¼ c. water. Add sugar, butter and salt to milk, cool. Mix eggs and yeast together, add to cooled mixture. Add 2 c. flour, mix well, gradually add remaining flour and let stand for 2 hours. Place on floured board and roll to about ¼ inch thickness. Spread with ¼ c. oleo, then sprinkle with sugar and cinnamon. Roll and cut in 1 inch slices. Place on greased baking sheets and let rise one hour. Bake in 350° degree oven approximately 30 minutes. Frost with Honey Topping.

HONEY TOPPING

1 tbsp. melted butter	1 tsp. vanilla	2 tbsp. cream
1 c. pow. sugar	Nut meats, finely chopped.	

—— Mrs. Howard (Esther) Miller

DINNER ROLLS

1 cake or pkg. dry yeast	1 tsp. salt	1 c. lukewarm water
3½ c. sifted flour (about)	½ c. milk	1 tbsp. sugar
2 tbsp. melted shortening or lard.		

Scald milk. Add sugar and salt. Cool to lukewarm. Dissolve yeast in lukewarm water. Add 2 mixtures together. Add ½ flour and beat well. Add melted shortening and rest of flour (or enough to make moderately firm dough) Knead well till smooth and elastic. Place in well greased bowl. Cover and let rise in warm place till double in bulk. (about 1½ hrs.) Shape into small rolls and place in well greased pans. Cover and let rise until light (about 40 min.) Beat the yolk of an egg and add 1 tbsp. milk. Dribble this mixture over rolls. Bake at 450° for 10 minutes.

——Mrs. Howard (Esther) Miller

DOUGHNUTS

5 c. warm water	4 pkg. dry yeast	2 c. sugar
4 beaten eggs	5 tsp. salt	1½ c. shortening
5 lb. flour		

"If you do a good deed for someone, and expect a good deed in return, it's not an act of kindness, it's only a trade."

DOUGHNUTS

½ c. shortening ½ c. sugar 1 tsp. salt
½ c. mashed potatoes 3 egg yolks
6½ c. flour 1½ pkg. yeast 1 pt. milk

Scald and cool milk. Blend shortening into sifted flour. Dissolve yeast in 1/3 c. warm water. Mix eggs, milk and sugar, salt, potatoes and yeast. Then add to flour mixture, mix thoroughly. Let rise 1 hour, roll out then let rise 1½ hours, then fry in deep hot fat. Glace with glaze made of 1 lb. powdered sugar, 4 tbsp. cream or milk, 2 tbsp. each of cornstarch, butter and vanilla. Add water to make paste (not too thin). Dip donuts in glaze and drain.

EASY ROLLS

1 c. lard or shortening, pour 1 c. boiling water over this to melt it. Cool to lukewarm. Now take 1 c. lukewarm water and dissolve 2 pkg. yeast in this. Pour into the lukewarm lard mixture and add 2 beaten eggs, ½ c. sugar and 1 tbsp. salt. Add enough flour for a soft dough, about 5 c. depending on the kind of flour. Roll them out right away and set in a warm place to rise about 1 to 1½ hours, and bake in a moderate oven. When cool, ice with powdered sugar icing. —— M.S.

GRAPE NUTS

7 c. whole wheat flour 4 c. buttermilk (or sweet milk with a little vinegar added) 1 c. sugar, 1 c. molasses. (Sorghum molasses is rich in iron and gives a good rich flavor.) 2 tsp. soda, 1 tsp. salt. Bake slowly till done. Then break or cut in pieces. Dry, then grind.

BLUEBERRY MUFFINS

¼ c. butter ¼ c. sugar 1 egg
1 c. milk 2 c. flour 4 tsp. baking pow.
½ tsp. salt ¾ c. drained blueberries.

Mix, do not over beat. Bake at 425 degrees. (Cranberries or other fruit is also good.)
  —— E. K. F., Arizona

"Most of us like people who come right out and say what they think——unless they disagree with us."

PANCAKE RECIPE

2 beaten eggs   ½ c. sugar   1 tsp. salt
5 tbsp. salad oil or melted butter   2 c. milk
2¼ c. flour   3 tbsp. baking powder (about)

Stir together sugar, salt, flour and baking powder. Add eggs, oil or butter and milk.
—— Howard Esther Miller

MOTHER'S PANCAKES

¾ cup flour   1 egg   pinch of salt
¼ tsp. soda   1 c. milk

Put first 4 ingredients in bowl. Do not stir until milk is added. Stir very little. Batter will be lumpy. If stirred too much, pancakes will be tough. Fry in skillet with small amount of grease. Makes about 8 average pancakes
—— Elizabeth Hilty

PANCAKE MIX

10 c. flour   5½ tbsp. baking pow.   ½ c. sugar
4 tsp. salt   2 c. dry milk.

Mix ingredients thoroughly, sifting together several times. Store in covered container at room temperature. Makes 12½ cups of mix.

PLAIN PANCAKES

3¼ cups mix   2 eggs
3 tbsp. melted lard   2 c. water or milk

POTATOE PANCAKES

1 egg   2 tbsp. melted butter   ½ c. milk
1 c. flour   1 c. grated potatoes   ¼ tsp. salt
2 tsp. baking pow.

Grate potatoes into a bowl and cover with egg. Milk and butter added next. Mix dry ingredients and sift. Stir liquid ingredients into dry ingredients. Beat well and cook on hot griddle.

"You can often tell when people are going to the dogs: They begin to unleash their emotions and make biting remarks."

PARKER HOUSE ROLLS

2 c. scalded milk   ½ c. wh. sugar   2 tsp. salt
3 tsp. shortening

Combine and cool until lukewarm, meanwhile, moisten 2 pkg. yeast in ¼ c. warm water. Warm and add 1 tsp. sugar and add to milk mixture. Add 2 beaten eggs, stir in 4 c. flour, beat thoroughly and add flour until it can no longer be stirred with a spoon. Let rise to double in bulk, can be used to make rolls, buns or donuts.

ZUCCHINI PANCAKES

2 c. grated uncooked squash   ½ c. flour
1 tsp. baking powder   1 egg, well beaten
salt   Butter or margarine for frying

Pat grated squash in bowl, add flour and baking powder, salt and then add beaten egg. Mix well. Fry as you would pancakes, making each about 2 to 3 inches in diameter. Makes 10 to 12, serve with honey or honey butter.

POT PIE

1 c. flour   ½ tsp. salt   1 tsp. baking pow.
1 tbsp. butter   ½ c. milk (scant)

Mix as for pie dough with a small amount of milk. Roll out on floured board about ¼ inch thick. Mark off in diamonds or squares and drop into simmering broth, or on top of cream chicken. Do not boil hard but simmer about 12 minutes without raising the lid of the pot. This can also be used as drop dumplings on top of sour kraut or excellent in beef broth.

—Mrs. D.Y.S., Bryant, Ind.

POT PIE OR DUMPLINGS

2½ c. sifted flour   1 tsp. baking pow.
½ tsp. salt   dash of pepper   ½ c. shortening

Mix all together like pie dough and mix until a soft ball is formed. Roll dough on a floured board about 1/8 thick, cut into 1" strips and these into 1" pieces. Drop into 2 qts. boiling chicken or beef broth. Cook slowly 15 to 20 minutes.

ROLLS, SUBS, or DOUGHNUTS

3 pkg. yest   1 c. lukewarm water   1 tsp. salt
¼ c. oleo   1 c. scalded milk   3 eggs
5 or 6 c. flour

    Pour scalded milk in bowl, over salt, 3 tbsp sugar and shortening. Meanwhile pour water over yeast and 1 tbsp. sugar, stir and let stand. When milk is lukewarm, add yeast and eggs and 3 c. flour, beat until smooth. Add 2 c. flour yet, or more. Beat or knead until dough is smooth. Dough must be stiff. Let rise in warm place until double in bulk. Knead down and let rise again. Shape into doughnuts or rolls, subs, and let rise again. Bake at 350° 20-25 minutes.
    ——Elizabeth Hilty

SPEEDIE ROLLS

½ c. sugar   2 eggs   1 tbsp. salt
1 or 2 pkg. yeast   1/3 c. shortening or butter
6½ c. flour.   2 c. warm water

    Place water, sugar, salt and yeast and 2 c. flour in mixing bowl, beat 2 minutes, add eggs and melt shortening, beat 1 minute. Gradually add 4½ c. flour, stir until dough is firm. Allow dough to set at least 20 minutes for ease in handling. Then roll, spread with melted butter, then sprinkle with sugar and cinnamon. Roll and cut. Put in greased pans and let rise. Bake in 375° oven 25-30 min. until done.
    ——Mrs. John Hilty

SPICY SUGAR LOAF

1 loaf white bread (1 lb.)   ¼ c. butter (I use oleo)
2/3 c. sugar   1 tsp. cinnamon

    Glaze: ½ c. sifted confectioners sugar, 1½ to 2 tbsp. light cream, 2 tbsp. finely chopped nuts.

    Spread bread slices on one side with softened butter; sprinkle with combined sugar and cinnamon. Put back in shape of loaf. Wrap loaf securely in foil and heat in moderate oven (375°) for 20 to 25 minutes. Unwrap, make glaze and pour glaze over top and sprinkle with nuts. Serve piping hot. Makes 10 to 12 servings. P.S. I make this a lot without the glaze.   ——V.J.S., Monroe, Ind.

"A man is rich according to what he gives, not what he has."

SWEET ROLLS OR DOUGHNUTS

In a mixing bowl put ½ c. scalded milk and ½ c. sugar, 1 tbsp. + ½ c. butter or oleo. When this mixture is luke warm and 2 pkgs. dry yeast dissolved in warm water, add 2 eggs slightly beaten. 1 c. flour, mix lightly, add 4 c. more flour when it is too stiff to use spoon, knead in, cover and let rise until double, about 1 hour. Knead down and roll out on floured board, form into roll or doughnuts. Let rise again for rolls. Bake in 375 degree oven. Fry doughnuts in deep fat.
——Mrs. John Hilty

CORN MEAL WAFFLES

½ c. sifted flour   1 tsp. baking pow.   ½ tsp. salt
1 tbsp. sugar   ½ c. corn meal   2/3 c. milk
¼ c. melted butter   2 eggs, separated.

Sift flour, baking powder, salt and sugar; add corn meal. Add milk and butter to beaten egg yolks, add to dry ingredients all at once. Mix well. Fold in stiffly beaten egg whites. Bake on hot waffle iron. Serve with butter and maple syrup. Yield: 3 waffles.
——Mrs. M.N.E., Bryant, Ind.

BANANA BREAD

1 c. sugar   ½ c. shortening   2 eggs
4 T. sour milk   2 c. flour   1 tsp baking soda
1 c. Mashed Bananas   ½ t. salt   1 c nuts (opt)

Cream sugar, eggs, and shortening. Add milk, and then dry ingredients. Pout into loaf pan and bake (350°) for 45 min. or until done.

"Before you begin to give some one a piece of your mind, consider carefully whether you can spare any."

"Wherever a man goes to dwell, his character goes too."

"A man is rich according to what he gives, not what he has."

MEAT DISHES

BEEF HEART (STUFFED)

3 to 3½ lb. beef heart   1 c. cracker crumbs
1 c. roasted chesnuts, coarsely chopped
½ c. white sauce   1 tsp. salt

    Mix together crumbs and chestnuts. Add white sauce until well blended. Stuff heart with mixture. Fasten with skewers. Place in Dutch oven. Cover with water and add salt. Cover and simmer until tender, about 2 hours. Remove heart from water ½ hour before serving and sprinkle with additional cracker crumbs, salt and pepper. Bake at 350° until browned. Carve crosswise into ½ in. slices.

BAKED CHICKEN LOAF (for weddings)

1 — 4 to 5 lb. chicken, cooked and cubed.
2 c. uncooked rice   2 c. chicken broth   4 eggs
2 c. bread cubes   2 c. milk   2 c. finely diced celery
Salt and pepper to taste.

    Mix all ingredients; place in a buttered casserole. Bake at 350° for 1 hour or until a kinife comes out clean as you test the center of the loaf. Serve in slices with chicken gravy. Yield: 20 servings.   ——M.N.E.

BARBECUE SAUCE

3 tbsp. butter   ½ c. minced onion   ¼ c. minced green
¾ c. catsup   2 tbsp. br. sugar   pepper
2 tbsp. mustard   1 tbsp. Worcestershire sauce
1 tbsp. salt

    Combine all ingredients; simmer for 15 minutes. Serve over meat. Yield: 1 cup.   ——Mrs. M.N.E., Bryant, Ind.

PENNSYLVANIA BOLOGNA

40 lbs. beef   1 lb. tender quick   1 Tbsp. black pepper
2 oz. ground Coriander seed   1 tsp. salt peter
½ tsp. garlic   10 lbs. sausage   8 pts. cold water
1 lb. salt   3 tbsp. liquid smoke   1 tsp. mace

    Grind meat and tender quick, salt and salt peter together. Let cure 24 hrs. Then mix the rest of the ingredients. Cold pack 3 hrs.
                 —— R.Y.S. Seymour, Mo.

CHICKEN or HAMBURG BOLOGNY

To make chicken bologny cut off meat from bones as for hamburg. To 25 lbs. of fresh chicken or hamburg, add 1 lb. tenderquick. Grind twice, let stand 24 hours. Then add the following:

½ c. sugar 1 oz. black pepper 2 tsp. salt peter
1 tsp. garlic salt 3 tbsp. smoke

Grind again. Mix well. Put in can and process 4 hours. This can be put in cloth bags, cooked and kept in ice box if used right away.

CREAMED CHICKEN

½ c. chopped celery 1½ tsp. chopped onion
1 tbsp. chopped green pepper
2 tbsp. fat ¼ c. flour 1½ c. chicken broth
½ c. milk or cream 1½ c. diced cooked chicken
Salt to taste.

Cook celery, onion and green pepper in hot fat until tender. Blend flour with fat and vegetable mixture. Stir in chicken broth and milk; cook until smooth; stirring constantly. Add chicken to sauce; season with salt. Heat thoroughly. Yield: 4 servings. —— M.N.E., Bryant, Ind.

FRENCH FRIED FRANKS

1½ c. pancake mix ½ tsp. salt ¼ tsp. chili powder
¼ tsp. dry mustard 1 tsp. grated onion.

Mix above in a bowl. Add 1 c. water and beat smooth. Dip franks in batter, drain excess and fry in deep fat or oil at 375° until golden brown—2 to 3 minutes.

HAM LOAF

1½ lbs. smoke house ham ½ lb. lean beef
¾ lb. fresh ham 1 c. bread crumbs
2 eggs beaten 1 No. 2 can tomatoes
½ tsp. mustard.

Mix all together. Form in loaf and stick 6 whole cloves on top. Bake in 400° oven until brown and reduce to 350°. Bake 1 hour.

HAM AND CHICKEN ROLL

½ boned chicken breast 1 slice ham about ¼" thick
1 slice Swiss cheese   Salt and Pepper
Sesame seed   Cracker crumbs.

Baste with 1 c. boiling water, 1 chicken bouillon cube, and 1 tsp. soy sauce. Flatten chicken breast, lay slice of ham and cheese on chicken and roll (like jelly roll), fasten with tooth picks. Beat egg. Dip chicken roll in egg, salt and pepper and sprinkle with sesame seed, then roll in cracker crumbs. Fry in vegetable shortening just until browned. About 1 hour before serving, mix water, bouillon cube and soy sauce together and pour over chicken. Bake in 350 degree oven. Baste about every 15 minutes.

BARBECUE HAMBURGERS

2 slightly beaten eggs 2 c. soft bread crumbs
2 tsp. salt   2 lb. hamburger
¼ c. minced onion   ¼ c. milk.

Combine above ingredients and mix well. Shape in thin patties. Broil over hot coals, brusing both sides with barbecue sauce. This is also a good recipe for meat loaf.
BARBECUE SAUCE: 2 tbsp. br. sugar, 2 tbsp. vinegar, 2 tbsp. Worcestershire sauce, 1 c. catsup.
— — Anna Beachy

G'SHTUPTAFUL LEW'R (STUFFED LIVER)

1 calf's liver (2 to 3 lbs.)   3 strips (8 oz.) salt pork
Bread stuffing   ½ c. flour   ½ tsp. salt
¼ tsp. pepper   ½ c. water

Rinse the liver in cold salted water. Drain thoroughly and wipe dry. Outside membrane should be removed. Make an incision in the thickest part. Lightly fill liver with bread stuffing. Fasten with skewers. Coat liver with a mixture of the flour, salt, and pepper. Place in roasting pan on rack and arrange strips of salt pork on top. Pour water into the pan. Cook in a 350° oven 1½ to 2 hr.
BREAD STUFFING. Soak 4 slices bread and squeeze dry. Lightly toss with a mixture of 1 tsp. salt, 1/8 tsp. pepper, and ¼ tsp. poultry seasoning. Mix in 1 tsp. chopped parsley and 1 tsp. grated onion. Add 2 tbsp. melted buter and 1 slightly beaten egg and toss lightly until thoroughly mixed.

LUNCHEON MEAT BARBECUE

Combine in a large frying pan:
1 can (8 oz.) tomato sauce ¼ c. br. sugar
3 tbsp. vinegar ½ tsp. salt ½ tsp. Wor. sauce
1 tsp. dry mustard, onion flakes and chili powder.

Simmer 5 min. Add 1 can (12 oz) luncheon meat and cut in 8 slices. Simmer 5 more minutes. Can be put into a baking dish, cutting almost thro' loaf, put drained peaches between. Put sauce over all and warm covered. Sweet potatoes are nice served around ham loaf.

PRESSURE COOKER MEAT BALLS

½ c. rice 1½ lb. ground beef 1 tsp. salt
½ tsp. pepper 1 tbsp. minced onion ½ c. water
1 sm. can tomato soup

Combine meat, rice, salt, pepper and onion. Shape into small balls. Heat tomato soup and water in pressure cooker. Drop meat balls in soup mixture. Cover. Cook for 10 minutes at 15 lbs. pressure. Yield: 6 servings.
—— Mrs. M.N.E., Bryant, Ind.

MEAT CURE (Amish recipe)

2 lbs. br. sugar 4 gal. water 6 lbs. salt
2 oz. pepper 1 oz. salt peter.

Bring to a boil. Cool. Pack meat in crock as close as possible. Put on a weight on top, leave ham in 4 weeks, bacon 5 days. Then smoke with hickory bark. Wrap in paper or cloth. Put in smoke house 1 week. Side and sausage 3 days.

MEAT LOAF

1 lb. gr. beef ½ lb. fresh gr. pork 1½ c. rolled oats
1 tbsp. ground or chopped onions 2 eggs beaten
1 tsp. salt ½ tsp. pepper 1 pt. tomatoes

Mix all ingredients except tomato juice. Baste with tomato juice and bake in moderate oven.

MEAT LOAF AND SAUCE

2/3 c. dry bread crumbs   1 c. milk
1½ lb. gr. beef   2 eggs slightly beaten   1 tsp. salt
¼ c. chopped onion 1/8 tsp. pepper   ½ tsp. sage

    Soak crumbs in milk, then add remaining ingredients. Cover loaf with sauce. Bake at 350° for 1 hour.
    PIQUANT SAUCE: Combine 3 tbsp. br. sugar, ¼ c. catsup, ¼ tsp. nutmeg, ¼ tsp. dry mustard.
    ——Mrs. Mennow W. Schwartz, Monroe, Ind.

CANNED MEAT MEAT LOAF

2 qt. canned hamburger   ½ lb. soda cracker crumbs
4 or 5 eggs   2 med. onions diced
Milk——enough to make the right consistency.

    Mix hamburger, eggs, crackers, onions and some milk. Mix well. Then add more milk if too thick. Also add a little salt and pepper if desired, or to suit taste. Mix well. Put in loaf pans. Add a few tbsp. cold water around edge of loaf. Bake in 375° oven for ½ hour or until browned on top and baked through. Catsup may be added when half done or when ready to serve.
    —— Mrs. M. N. E., Bryant, Ind.

MEAT LOAF

1½ lbs. gr. beef   ¾ c. rolled oats (uncooked)
1½ tsp. salt   ¼ c. chopped onion   ¼ tsp. pepper
1 egg beaten   ¾ c. milk
SAUCE: 1/3 c. catsup, 2 tbsp. br. sugar, 1 tbsp. mustard
    Heat oven to moderate (350°). Combine all ingredients. Mix thoroughly. Pack firmly into loaf pan. Combine all ingredients for sauce and pour over meat loaf. Bake in preheated oven about 1 hr. Let stand 5 min. before slicing.   —— J. J. S., Monroe, Ind.

"Yesterday cannot be recalled. Tomorrow cannot be assured. Only today is certain."

MEAT LOAF

1½ lb. gr. beef	1 c. tomato juice	¾ c. oatmeal
2 eggs	¼ c. onion, cut fine	salt, pepper to taste

    Mix all ingredients and place in casserole. Bake. When half done, mix and spread on top, 2 tsp. mustard, 4 tbsp. catsup and 4 tbsp. br. sugar. If too thick, add a little water. When done remove from oven, leave set 5 min. before cutting.

ROLLED STUFFED MEAT LOAF

1 lb. gr. beef	¼ lb. bulk sausage	½ tsp. salt
1 egg	3 c. bread crumbs	2 tbsp. ch. onion
2 tbsp. ch. parsley	1/3 c. water	1 tbsp. sugar
1/8 tsp. sage	1/8 tsp. pepper	¼ c. ch. celery
¼ c. melted butter		

    Combine beef, sausage, salt and egg and chill while making the stuffing by combining the rest of the ingredients. Mix stuffing thoroughly. Spread meat mixture onto waxed paper, making rectangle about ½" thick, and about 9 x 12". Place stuffing in a 9" roll across center of meat. Bring waxed paper over ends of meat, overlap 2". Peel off paper and place in baking dish or pan so that the joint is on the bottom. Place strip of bacon on top. Bake in 375° oven for one hour. Baste every 10 to 15 minutes with 1 c. evaporated milk diluted with 1 c. water.

MEAT PIE

1 lb. gr. beef	¼ c. bread crumbs	¼ c. ch. onions
¼ tsp. gr. pepper	1 tsp. salt	

    Mix above ingredients together. Press against sides and bottom of 9 inch pan. Then take 1 1/3 c. quick minute rice, 1½ c. tomato sauce (8 oz. can), 1 c. water and 1 cup grated cheese and mix. Pour into the meat lined pan. Bake for 45 min. at 350°.

MEXICAN PORK CHOPS

Fry about 8 pork chops till brown on both sides. Take ½c catsup, ¼ c. br. sugar, 1 c. water. Pour over pork chops. Cover and bake till tender, about 40 minutes.

PON HOSS

3 to 4 lb. pork shanks or hocks.   Corn meal
Salt and Pepper.

    Cook pork until tender. Remove bones. Skim fat from broth. Return meat to broth, and add corn meal to thicken. Season with salt and pepper. Chill. Slice and fry.
    —— M.N.E., Bryant, Ind.

POOR MAN'S STEAK

2 lb. hamburger   2 c. cracker crumbs   2 c. milk
Add onions, salt and pepper to suit taste.

    Mix and press into a large flat pan. Let set overnight. Then cut in squares, roll in flour, fry until brown. Put in casserole and put 1 can cream of mushroom soup (diluted with 1 can water) over top of meat and bake slowly for 2 hours. It is necessary to have this set overnight to make it firm.

BAKED POTATO AND SAUSAGE

    Take medium size potato, peel and cut small hole in center. Slip small piece of fresh link sausage through hole. Salt and pepper, put enough water to start baking. Cook until done.

CANNED SAUSAGE

1 gal. water   ½ c. salt   ½ c. sugar
1 tsp. pepper   1 tsp. salt peter

    Bring to boil. Add meat. Boil 20 minutes, then pack in jars and cover with liquid. Seal cold pack. 20 minutes, 10 lb. pressure.

SLOPPY JOES

1 lb. gr. beef   2 tbsp. cooking oil   1 c. ch. onions
1 lb. can pork & beans   1 c. barbecue sauce
2 tbsp. br. sugar   1 tsp. prepared mustard

    Brown beef in oil. Add onions and saute until tender. Add beans, barbecue sauce, sugar and mustard. Simmer covered for 10 minutes. ——Mrs. Marvin Hilty, Berne, Ind.

SLOPPY JOES

Finely chop and cook together:
    1 c. celery   ½ c. onion   ½ c. green pepper
Brown 1 lb. hamburger. Add vegetables, 1 can tomato soup, and 1 can cream of mushroom soup. Simmer 1 hour.

SLOPPIE JOE BURGERS

1 tbsp. lard   1 lg. onion   1 lb. hamburger
    Fry this until brown, then add:
1 tbsp. sugar   1 tbsp. dry mustard   ¾ c. catsup
1 tsp. salt   1 green pepper if you like
    Let cook slowly for ½ hr. before serving.

SKILLET SUPPER

1 lb. hamburger   4 tbsp. shortening   4 med. potatoes
4 med. carrots   ¾ c. pet milk   2 med. onions
1½ tsp. salt   1/8 tsp. pepper   1 c. water

Brown hamburger slowly in skillet with shortening. Put vegetables through medium knife of food chopper, then add to ground meat along with salt, pepper and water. Cover and cook slowly 20 minutes or until vegetables are tender. Stir occasionally, then add pet milk and continue cooking uncovered about 3 minutes longer or until thick. 8 servings.
    —— Mrs. David Y. Schwartz

STEAK ROLL UP WITH NOODLES

1½ lbs. flank steak   ½ c. ch. onion   3 tbsp. margarine
½ tsp. thyme   2 tsp. salt   ¼ tsp. sage
¼ tsp. pepper   ¼ tsp. basil   1 tsp. chili powder
1 clove garlic   1 No. 2½ can tomatoes
1 6 oz. can tomato paste

"Labor for God and others is the rent we pay for our room on earth."

"A hundred men make an encampment, but it takes a mother to make a home."

STEAK AND NOODLES

1½ lbs. sirloin steak 2 tbsp. cooking oil 2 cans mushroom soup
1 - 8 oz. can mushrooms, stems and pieces. Do not drain.
½ c. sherry cooking wine (optional)
1 lg. pk. medium sized noodles boiled according to directions.

Cut the steak in thin strips leaving no fat or gristle. Saute steak in the hot oil 15 minutes, stirring meat the while. (A liquid will form on the meat which is all right). Add mushroom soup and undrained mushrooms and cook for 10 to 15 minutes. Add the cooking wine and serve over cooled noodles. (The noodles can be cooked as the meat concoction is being prepared.

SUGAR CURE FOR MEAT

3 c. salt   1 c. br. or wh. sugar
½ tbsp. salt petre   1 tbsp. pepper.

Mix together, then put over meat, rubbing well in around bone. Repeat in 10 days and again in 10 days.

WIGGLERS

1½ lb. hamburger   1½ c. ch. celery   1½ c. cut up carrots
1 can cream of mushroom soup   1½ ch. onions
1½ c. cut up potatoes   1 can peas
1 pkg. small spaghetti.   9 slices bacon, fried.

Add Velvetta cheese, pour on top. Fry hamburger and onion in bacon grease. Put all together in big roaster. Bake 1½ hours, in 350° oven. Add bacon and cheese only last half hour.

YIPS YIPS for LARGE CROWD (120)

10 lb. hamburger   Salt to taste   2 lg. ch. onions
1 lg. green pepper, diced   1 stalk celery finely chopped
1 qt. barbecue sauce   2 bottles catsup   10 doz. buns

Combine meat, salt, onions, pepper and celery. Cook until meat is done. Add barbecue sauce and catsup. Cook slowly about 1 hr. Serve on buns.
—— M.N.E., Bryant, Ind.

"Each day we live we make memories for tomorrow; now is the time to do away with future nightmares."

SOUPS
Casseroles

BEEF NOODLE SOUP

3 lb. beef chunks	butter	1 tsp. sweet basil
1 tsp. parsley flakes	2 med. onions, ch.	4 carrots diced
2 celery hearts diced		2 No. 2 cans mashed tomatoes
8 qt. water	2 tsp. sugar	1 lb. noodles. (homemade)
Salt and pepper to taste		

Brown beef in butter with basil, parsley flakes and onion. Then simmer for 5 min. Add tomatoes, carrots and celery. Add water and sugar. When liquid boils, reduce heat. Simmer for 2½ hours or until meat is tender. Add noodles, salt and pepper during last 8 minutes. 16 servings.

M.N.E., Bryant, Ind.

BEEF VEGETABLE SOUP

2 lbs. stew beef	6 qt. water	6 carrots ch.
4 potatoes ch.	1 med. onion ch.	2 stalks celery ch.
1 sm. cabbage ch.	1 No. 2 can tomatoes	Salt & pepper
1 lb. med. noodles.		

Place beef in large pan, add water. Cook until beef is half done. Add vegetables and seasonings. Continue cooking for 1½ hours or until vegetables are done. Add more liquid of necessary. Add noodles, cook until tender. Yield: 6 to 8 servings.

Mrs. M.N.E., Bryant, Ind.

BRAUNE MEHLSUPPE (Brown Flour Soup)

¼ c. butter	½ c. flour	5 c. soup stock
Salt	Pepper	Grated cheese.

Melt butter, blend in flour, heat until bubbly. Remove from heat, cool, add the cooled stock slowly, stir, add salt and pepper. Cook low heat 20 min. Sprinkle with cheese when serving.

CABBAGE CHOWDER SOUP

4 c. shredded cabbage	2 c. sliced carrots	1 tbsp. salt
3 c. diced potatoes	½ tsp. pepper	3 c. water
4 c. scalded milk	2 tbsp. butter	½ tsp. sugar

Cook vegetables, seasonings and water till tender. Add 4 c. scalded milk and 2 tbsp. butter. Serve with crackers.

—— M.M.S., Etna Green, Ind.

CHILLIE SOUP

1 lb. hamburger   1 qt. cooked navy beans or kidney beans
1 c. tomatoes   1 ch. onion (or more)
1 tsp. chili powder   Salt   Pepper

Fry hamburger, onion, add to beans, tomatoes and seasonings. Simmer 1 hour. Add water to make right thickness. Add brown sugur to suit your taste.

HEINZ TOMATO SOUP

2 lg. stalks celery   2 lg. onions   ½ bu. tomatoes

Cook and strain, then add:

1 c. sugar   2 red peppers   1 c. flour
½ c. salt   1 c. butter.

Make paste with tomato juice or water and cook 15 minutes and can.   —— Mrs. Howard Miller

ONE POT MEAL

2½ lbs. ham (approx.)   1 qt. snapped green beans
diced potatoes   Salt and pepper to taste.

Place ham in large pot, cover with water. Cook slowly for about 2 hrs. Add water when necessary to prevent dryness. Put beans in pot with ham, also potatoes, cook slowly for 25 minutes or until tender. Season to taste. 6 servings.
    —— M.N.E., Bryant, Ind.

RIVEL SOUP

1 qt. chicken broth   1 c. flour   ¼ tsp. salt
1 egg well beaten   1 c. whole kernel corn, crushed

Bring the broth to a boil. Combine flour, salt, and egg until mixture is crumbly. Rub through hands into the boiling broth and add the corn and cook about 10 minutes. The rivels look like boiled rice when cooked.

TOMATOE COCKTAIL

½ bu. tomatoes   4 mangoes   4 onions
1 bunch celery   6 cloves

Cook together till tender, put through sieve. Add 2 c. sugar, ¼ c. salt, 3 lemons (juice). Cold pack 20 minutes. To use as a soup, you can add a corn starch sauce.   ——C.E.S., Geneva, Ind.

TOMATO SOUP (to can)

½ bu. tomatoes   12 onions   2 stalks celery
1 stalk parsley   2 or 3 mangoes   2 c. flour
2 c. sugar   ½ c. salt   lump of butter
small amount of milk.

Cook tomatoes, onions, parsley, celery and mangoes. Add flour, sugar and salt. Heat almost to boiling, put in cans and cold pack 1 hour. When serving a lump of butter and small amount of milk is very good with this.

CASSEROLES

BARBECUED BEANS

1 lb. Hamburger   1 lb. 12 oz. can pork and beans
1 tbsp. vinegar   ½ c. ch. onion   ½ c. catsup
1 tbsp. Wor. sauce Salt   Pepper.

Add a little brown sugar and just a little chili powder. Brown meat and onions together. Pour off fat. Add remaining ingredients. Bake for 30 minutes.

BEEF AND MACARONI BAKE

¾ lb. gr. chuck   ¼ c. finely ch. onion   1½ tsp. salt
1/3 c. bread crumbs 1/8 tsp. pepper   1 tbsp. water
1/3 c. tomato sauce 1 tsp. Wor. sauce.   1/3 c. water
1 - 10½ can condensed tomato soup.
1 c. shredded American cheese   4 oz. cooked elbo macaroni

Mix first 8 items. Then mix soup and water and heat. Blend cheese in the soup and water, stirring until melted. Add to meat mixture. Press 1/3 of meat mixture in a greased 1½ qt. casserole. Cover with macaroni. Top with rest of meat. Bake at 350° 45 to 50 minutes.

CHEESE OMELET

2 tbsp. melted butter 3 tbsp. flour   ½ tsp. soda
¼ c. cheese cut fine   2 eggs beaten   ½ c. scalded milk

Mix the ingredients and bake at 350° for 50 or 55 minutes.

SCALLOPED CARROTS

10 carrots
½ c. cream
3 tbsp. butter
1 c. bread crumbs
½ c. milk
3 eggs separated.
½ c. ch. onion
Salt & pepper

Peel and slice carrots; boil until soft. Drain and mash. Combine with other ingredients except egg whites. Place in casserole; top with beaten egg whites. Bake at 350° for 30 minutes. Note: 3 whole eggs may be beaten and combined with other ingredients if topping is not desired.
Mrs. M. N. E.

COMPANY CASSEROLE

1½ lb. gr. chuck
1 tsp. seasoned salt
1 can peas undrained
1 can condensed tomato soup
1 8 oz. pkg. spaghetti (elbo) cooked
3 sm. onions, ch.
pepper to taste
1 tsp. salt
1 can mushroom (pieces)
½ green pepper (diced)

Mix all together and bake in a greased casserole at 350° about one hour.

BAKED CORN

3 eggs added to a pint of creamed corn
1½ c. milk   Salt to taste
1 tbsp. corn starch
2 tbsp. sugar

Combine all together and bake at 350° about one hour in a greased casserole.

BAKED CORN

2 c. canned corn
1 c. milk
1/8 tsp. pepper
2 tbsp. crisco or oleo
1 tbsp. sugar
2 eggs
1½ c. flour
1 tsp. salt

Mix all together. Bake at 325° to 350° until firm.

BAKED SWEET CORN

1 qt. sweet corn
1 tbsp. flour
sugar and salt to suit.
2 beaten eggs
½ c. sweet cream
1 c. crumbled crackers
celery leaves

Mix all together. Grease pan, bake at 350° for 30 minutes or until done.

——Mary Ann Troyer, Apple Cree, Ohio

GREEN BEANS WITH BACON

1½ lb. green beans cleaned   8 slices thick bacon cut in pcs.
½ small onion   1 tsp. salt

    Simmer all ingredients together in water until beans are tender and bacon is fully cooked.

HAM VEGETABLE CASSEROLE

1 - 10½ oz. can condensed cream of mushroom soup
½ c. milk   1/3 c. ch. onion   2 c. diced potatoes
1 c. sliced carrots   1 - 10 oz. pkg. frozen lima beans, thawed
1½ c. cooked ham, cut in strips
½ c. buttered soft bread crumbs.

    Mix soup and milk; heat to boiling, stirring; add vegetables alternately with ham to fill greased 1½ qt. casserole. Sprinkle bread crumbs over top. Bake in moderate oven 350° for one hour. Makes 6 servings.

          V.J.S.   Monroe, Ind.

HOMINY

2 qts. shelled corn   2 tbsp. lye   2 gal. water.

    Cook for ½ hour, if the eyes don't come off, cook longer. Wash corn and rinse often. Let stand over night, then can. Do not fill cans as kernels get again as large.

HAMBURGER CASSEROLE

2 lb. gr. beef browned   6 med. potatoes sliced
2 med. onions sliced   2 cans mushroom soup
1 c. water

    Put a layer of each in baking dish. Cover and bake at 350° until potatoes are tender. About 1½ hours.

HAMBURGER CASSEROLE

2 lb. hamburger   1 ch. onion ------brown together
1 pkg. 8 oz. noodles fine or medium, cooked.
1 pt. peas, cooked   1 can cr. of chicken soup
2 cans cream mushroom soup   1 c. sour milk
Salt and pepper to suit taste.

    Mix and put buttered bread crumbs on top. Bake until brown.

      —— Mrs. John Henry Yoder, Virginia Beach, Va.

KING RANCH CHICKEN

1 boiled, boned chicken   1 pkg. tortillos, cut in ¼s
   Saute in butter, onion, green peppers, celery
Mix: 1 can Rotel tomatoes   1 can creamed chicken soup
   1 can mushroom soup   1 can cheese soup
   salt and pepper to taste.
Layer in casserole and sprinkle cheese on top. Bake at 350° till a little brown on top and bubbly.

NOODLE CASSEROLE

2 lb. hamburger, add salt   1 qt. cooked noodles, add salt
1 qt. potatoes, cut up, add salt   1 qt. green beans or peas.
2 cans cream of mushroom soup.
   Lightly brown meat in skillet, then preboil noodles, potatoes and green beans, then add soup to noodles and mix together, add layers of meat, potatoes, noodles and beans in roaster. Bake at 350°.

MEAT NOODLE CASSEROLE

1 - 8 oz. pkg. noodles   ¾ lb. hamburger   2 sm. onions, ch.
1 - 10 oz. can tomato soup   1/8 tsp. Wor. sauce
½ c. grated American cheese   2 c. diced celery
1 small green pepper, chopped
   Cook noodles in boiling salt water. Drain and rinse. Brown meat in hot fat, add onion, celery and green pepper. Cook until tender, season. Alternate meat and noodles in greased casserole. Pour over soup mixed with Worcestershire sauce. Sprinkle with cheese. Bake 45 minutes at 325°. Serves 8.   ——Mrs. Dan D. (Leah) Schwartz

POTATO PUFFS

1 c. left over mashed potatoes   1 or 2 eggs
¼ tsp. salt   ¼ to ½ c. flour   1 tsp. baking pow.
   Mix well and drop by tablespoons in deep fat. Fry until brown.

SQUASH PATTIES

3 c. ground summer squash   1 egg
1 c. flour   2 tsp. baking pow.   ½ c. milk
   Salt and pepper to taste. Fry in patties.

SEVEN LAYER CASSEROLE

Fill a 2 qt. baking dish, greased, with the following in order:
1 c. uncooked rice
1 c. whole kernel corn (drained with salt and pepper)
1 can tomato sauce and ½ can water
½ c. each chopped onion and green pepper
1 lb. uncooked ground beef, salt and pepper lightly
1 can tomato sauce and ¼ can water
4 strips of bacon cut in halves.

Cover and bake 1 hour. Uncover and bake ½ hour longer at 325° to 350°.

TUNA CASSEROLE

2 cans tuna   1 can mushroom soup
½ c. milk   crushed potato chips

Blend tuna, soup and milk in a casserole dish. Cover with crushed chips. Bake uncovered for ½ hour at 350°.

—— Mrs. David Y. S.

YUMINOSETTI (a large batch)

1 lb. noodles, cook in salt water
3 lb. hamburger, fry in butter with 1 onion
2 cans mushroom soup
1 can cream of chicken or celery soup
1 pt. peas and 1 c. sour cream.

Mix all the soups and cream together and pour over the other indgredients which have been put in a large container. Mix all together, put into roaster or large pans and bake in oven for one hour at 350°.

Our Talk

"Our talk ain't so for fanciness
   But plain, it makes just right.
It ain't so good dressed up in print,
   But from the heart it comes out bright."

"See that your kitchen fire be bright
And your hands be neat and skilled
For the love of man oft takes its flight,
If his stomach be not well filled."

SALADS
Pickles
Relishes

APPLE SALAD

Mix 1 egg   ½ c. sugar   1 tbsp. flour
½ c. water   Butter size of a walnut   1 tsp. vinegar

    Bring to a boil stirring briskly till mixture thickens, cool and mix with 4 bananas mashed, 6 apples diced and sugared and ½ c. nut meats.

BEAN SALAD

1 can cut green beans   1 can yellow beans (cut)
1 can kidney beans, washed and drained
1 can small lima beans, drained   ½ c. diced celery
½ c. cut green peppers   1 onion diced

    Mix this all together, then mix the following: 2/3 c. red wine vinegar, 1/3 c. salad oil, ¾ c. white sugar, 1 tsp. salt and pepper to taste. Stir until sugar dissolves and pour over beans. Chill several hours.

CABBAGE SALAD

Shred one large head of cabbage, 1 pepper and 2 med. onions
Then marianate 24 hours in the following:
1½ c. sugar   ¾ c. vinegar   ¾ c. salad oil
1 tbsp. salt. (Bring this to a boil, but do not boil)

    Pour over cabbage, mix well, cool and store in covered bowls in refrigerator.

    —— Mrs. N. N. Miller, Topeka, Ind.

CABBAGE SLAW RELISH

8 qt. gr. cabbage   4 qt. ground tomatoes   9 lb. gr. mangoes
10 lb. gr. onions   Add 1 c. salt and let stand over night.
    Wash and drain well.
    Add: 4 c. vinegar   2 c. water   1 tbsp. celery seed
         6 c. sugar   2 tbsp. mustard seed
Boil rapidly for 3 minutes. Put in jars and seal at once.

CRANBERRY SALAD

1 lb. cranberries   1 whole orange   2 apples
    Grind together, then add
1 c. sugar and mix well. Let set ½ to 1 hour. Dissolve 1 box cherry jello as directions and add to fruit mixture. When almost set, add 1 c. diced celery, ½ c. nuts chopped and 1½ c. of halved & seeded red grapes.

DANDELION SALAD

Dandelion greens, washed and dried.
4 thick slices bacon, cut into small pieces
¼ c. butter   ¼ c. half & half   2 eggs beaten
1 tsp. salt   pepper to taste   Paprika, optional
1 tbsp. sugar   ¼ c. cider vinegar

Heap greens in serving bowl and set in a warm place, such as near the stove. Fry bacon until crisp and pour it and the drippings over the greens. Add butter and cream to skillet and warm mixture over low heat. Beat eggs in a small bowl and blend in vinegar, sugar and seasonings. Pour this egg-vinegar mixture into the cream mixture in the skillet. Increase heat and cook until thickened, stirring constantly. Pour over greens and toss. Serve immediately.

FRUIT SALAD

1 sm. jar Mar. cherries   1 qt. peaches   1 qt. chunk pineapple
2 lbs. red grapes   2 lbs. green grapes
1 c. sugar   3 c. syrup from fruit
2 pkg. gelatine, soaked in 1 c. water

Bring sugar and juice to a boil, a few minutes, add few drops of yellow cake color and gelatin. Pour over fruit, drained well. Juice of 2 lemons and pour over 3 lbs. of sliced bananas and add to above fruit mixture. Keeps bananas from turning brown. Very good.

FRUIT SALAD

2 c. red or white grapes   2 c. pineapple tid-bits
2 c. mandarin oranges   24 small marshmallows
Cook the following until thick:
3 egg yolks   2 tbsp sugar   dash salt
2 tbsp. pineapple juice 1 tbsp. butter   2 tbsp. vinegar

Add this to the fruit, and chill several hours. Serve with whipped cream or whipped topping.

MANGO KRAUT

2 gal. shredded cabbage   1 qt. mangoes red & green, cut fine
2 tbsp. salt over above, mix well. Let stand ½ hr. Press dry
5 c. sugar   2 tbsp. mustard seed   2 pt. vinegar
2 tbsp. celery seed.

Heat to dissolve sugar. Pour over cabbage. Can put in pint containers and freeze or keep in refrigerator.

ISLAND DELIGHT SALAD

2 pkg. lemon jello   2 c. boiling water   2 c. cold water
No. 2 can crushed pineapple   3 sliced bananas
3 apples diced

    Dissolve Jello, drain and reserve juice from pineapple, add fruits to cooled jello. Chill.

TOPPING: 2 tbsp. flour   1 egg
½ c. sugar   1 c. fruit juice

    Blend sugar, blend flour, add juice and egg. Beat until smooth and cook over low heat, stirring constantly until thickened, cool. Fold in 1 c. whipped cream or Dream Whip and spread over jello.   —— Anna Beachy

WILTED LETTUCE (with bacon)

5 slices bacon, diced, cook until crisp
1 beaten egg   ¼ c. minced onion (optional)
2 tbsp. sugar   ½ tsp. salt   1/3 c. vinegar
2 tbsp. water   lettuce

    Combine egg, onion, sugar, salt, vinegar, and water. Add to bacon and drippings. Heat just until boiling stirring constantly. Pour over leaf lettuce or torn pieces of head lettuce (6 c. approximately) and toss lightly. Serves 4 at once.

PICKLED PEPPERS

1 part vinegar   2 parts water   3 parts sugar

    Stuff peppers with shredded cabbage. Pack in jars and fill with syrup and seal. Bring to a boil in water.

PEAR AND GRAPE SALAD

    Place pear halves, cut side down on lettuce. Spread with cream cheese then arrange seed grape halves close together on cheese to represent a bunch of grapes. Garnish with French dressing.

DILL PICKLES

5 qts. boiling water   1 qt. vinegar   1 2/3 c. salt

    Pack pickles in can with dill and a piece or so of garlic or garlic salt, ½ tsp. plus 1 tsp. alum. Pour on boiling hot and seal. (I usually cold pack just enough to seal)
    —— A. L. WISE

HEINZ SWEET PICKLES

7 lbs. pickles, washed and sliced. Soak 5 days in salt water that will float an egg (1 pt. salt to 1 gal. water). I use coarse salt. Drain and soak 2 days in clear water. Drain and cover with boiling water and 2 tbsp. powdered alum. Let stand 24 hours. Drain and cover with boiling water, let stand until cold or next day. Drain and cover with hot syrup. Do this 3 mornings. Cook syrup about 5 minutes each morning, then can. This syrup boils over easily, so be careful.

SYRUP: 3 pts. vinegar, 4 tbsp. allspice berries, 5 lbs. sugar, 4 tbsp. cinnamon bark, 4 tbsp. celery seed. Very good.   –– From mother and Savilla

MIXED PICKLES

1 qt. small onions   1 qt. lima beans   6 sweet peppers
1 qt. carrots cut up 1 qt. celery cut up   (cut up fine)
1 qt. bean soup (or dry kidney)   1 qt. green beans cut up
2 qt. tiny green pickles

Prepare, wash all vegetables, cut green beans in 1 inch pieces. Place beans, peppers, onions in enough cold salt water to cover (½ c. salt to 1 gal. water), let stand over night, drain. Cook each vegetable separate, not too done, about 10 minutes. 2 qt. vinegar, 4 c. sugar, 2 tbsp. mustard seed, 1 tbsp. pepper corn, 1 tsp. tumeric powder. Boil this together 10 minutes, add vegetables, boil 10 minutes longer. Pack in jars and seal. Let stand 6 weeks before using.

COMPANY BEST PICKLES

10 med. cucumbers   2 tbsp. mixed pickling spice
8 c. sugar   5 tbsp. salt   4 c. cider vinegar

Cover whole cucumbers with boiling water. Allow to stand until next morning. Drain. repeat this for 3 mornings. On fifth day, drain and slice in ½ in. slices.

Combine sugar, spices, salt and vinegar. Bring to boiling and pour over cucumbers. Let stand 2 days, on third day bring to boiling again and seal in hot sterilized jars.
   –– Mrs. John K. Schwartz, Berne, Indiana

"Choice, not chance will determine your destiny."

OLD FASHIONED POTATO SALAD

3 strips bacon chopped and browned. Add tsp. flour, little vinegar, salt and sugar to taste, also little water. Simmer few minutes then add to bowl of chopped cooked potatoes and green onions.

RIBBON SALAD

1 pkg. each (3 oz.) lemon, lime and Raspberry Jello. Dissolve flavors separately, using 1 c. boiling water for each. STir 1 c. miniature marshmallows into lemon and set aside. Add ¾ c. cold water to lime. Pour into a 9 x 13 x 2 inch pan. Chill until set, but not firm. Add ¾ c. cold water to raspberry, set aside at room temperature. Then add 2 pkgs. (3 oz) cream cheese, softened, to lemon mixture, beat until blended and chill until slightly thickened. Then blend in 1 c. whipped cream, ½ c. Mayonaise and 1 can (1 lb. 4½ oz.) crushed pineapple. Chill until thickened, spoon gently over lime gelatin. Chill raspberry gelatin until thickened. Pour over lemon, chill until firm. Makes about 10 cups, or 12 to 15 servings.
 ——Mrs. Amos Yoder, Kenton, Ohio

HOME MADE SALAD DRESSING

2 eggs	2/3 c. sugar	½ c. white vinegar
2 tbsp. butter	½ tsp. salt	few grains pepper
1 tsp. dry mustard.		

Beat eggs, then add sugar, vinegar, butter, salt, pepper and mustard. Cook until thickened and clear. While hot, pour over garden lettuce just to coat lettuce leaves, for wilted salad. May also be used cold in place of mayonaise for salads. Makes 1 cup.

FRENCH DRESSING

4 tsp. grated onion	3 tsp. salt	2 c. sugar
2 c. Wesson oil	1 c. vinegar	¼ c. lemon juice
2 tsp. paprika		

TOSSED SALAD DRESSING

4 tsp. grated onion	4 tsp. salt	2 c. sugar
1 c. Wesson oil	1 c. vinegar	1 1/3 c. catsup
¼ c. lemon juice	2 tsp. paprika	

—— Mrs. Dan N. Yoder, Apple Cree, Ohio

FRENCH DRESSING

1 can condensed tomato soup 3 c. sugar
1 tsp. salt 1 tsp. pepper 1 tsp. paprika
1 tsp. celery salt 1 tbsp. grated onion 1 c. vinegar
2 c. salad oil.

Makes ½ gallon. Combine all ingredients and mix well.
—— Melinda A. Hilty, Monroe, Ind.

TEN DOLLAR SALAD DRESSING

1 tsp. celery seed 1 tsp. dry mustard 1 tsp. salt
1 tsp. paprika 1 tbsp. grated onion ½ c. sugar
¼ c. vinegar 1 c. Wesson oil

Mix all except the oil. Add oil slowly while beating. Let stand 24 hours.

SANDWICH SPREAD

3 lg. onions 3 red mangoes 1 bunch celery
3 lg. carrots 3 green mangoes 3 ground cucumbers

(put 2 tbsp. salt on cucumbers and let stand 2 hrs., then drain.) Grind all but celery. (cut celery up fine). Then add: 1½ c. vinegar (diluted) 2c. sugar, 4 rounding tbsp. flour, 1 c. mustard. Cook slowly 25 min., stirring. Add ¼ lb. butter, cool slightly and add 1 pt. salad dressing. Then can.
——— S. S. S.

SANDWICH SPREAD

Grind: 6 red peppers 6 green peppers 6 onions
6 pickles 6 green tomatoes 1 pt. cut celery

Add: 2 handsful salt, let soak 2 hrs, drain. Boil this in 1 qt. vinegar and 1 pt. water. Mix 2 c. sugar, 1 pt. vinegar, 1 c. flour. Stir into mixture, keep stirring. Last add 1 pt. mustard. Can and seal. —— E.K.F., Arizona

SANDWICH SPREAD

12 green tomatoes 3 med. onions 12 red or green mangoes.
Grind and drain. Then mix:
2½ c. sugar 1 tsp. salt 1 c. mustard
1 tsp. celery seed.

Cook all together 10 minutes. Then add 1 qt. miracle whip. Let come to boil, and put in jars and seal at once.

THREE LAYER SALAD

2 boxes jello, lime and lemon   3¾ c. hot water
1 c. drained crushed pineapple
    Let stand until firm.
1 lg. pkg. cream cheese
1 c. cream whipped and sweetened, whipped again with the cheese. Spread on top of first layer.
1 c. sugar   2 tbsp. flour   2 eggs
1 c. pineapple juice.
    Cook till thick, put on top when ready to serve.

RARE SLAVE COOK RECIPE OF THE 1800's.

RESIPEE FOR CUKIN KON-FEEL PEES

Gether your pees 'bout sun-down. The foluin day, 'bout leven o'clock, gowge out your pees with your thum nale, like gowgin out a man's eye-ball at a kote house. Rense your pees, parbile them, then fry'em with some several slices uf streekt middlin, incouragin uv the gravy to seep out and intermarry with your pees. When modritly brown, but not scorcht, empty intoo a dish. Mash'em gently with a spune, mix with raw tomarters sprinkled with a little brown shugar and the immortal dish ar quite ready. Eat a hepe. Eat mo and mo. It is good for your general helth uv mind and body. It fattens you up, makes you sassy, goes throo and throo your very soul. But why don't you eat? Eat on. By Jings. Eat. Stop! Never, while thar is a pee in the dish.   —— Moses Addums

"Act right and you won't get left out at the Pearly Gates."

"A short snooze for an oldster in a favorite rocking chair is a generation nap."

"Some persons have a lot of good in them, mainly because they have not distributed much of it so far."

"To have what we want is riches, but to be able to do without is power."

JAMS
Jellies
Miscellaneous

APPLE CIDER APPLE BUTTER

3 gal. cider: cook down to ½, then add 1½ gal. apples. Cook till soft then, cook down ½ again. Add 5 lbs. sugar. Cook about 1½ hrs. or till thick enough. Scum cider while cooking. Put thru sieve. I usually cook in stainless steel cooker. Makes 6 qts.

CORN COB SYRUP

Boil 6 red corn cobs, washed for 1 hour in 3 quarts of water, strain then add 3 lbs. brown sugar and water enough to make 3 quarts. Boil until thick like syrup.

ARTIFICIAL HONEY

5 lbs. sugar	1½ pts. water	1 tsp. alum
12 red rose petals	8 pink rose petals	20 wh. clover blossoms

Dissolve sugar in water, boil until clear which will not take long. Then add alum and boil 2 minutes longer. Take from fire and add clover blossoms and petals and let stand 10 min. Strain in glasses. Cover with parafin.
   ––– Mrs. Jacob Schwartz, Seymour, Mo.

MULBERRY AND RHUBARB CONSERVE

3 c. mullberries   3 c. rhubarb   4 c. sugar
   Cook until thick.

RHUBARB JAM

5 c. rhubarb   5 c. sugar
   Boil 3 to 5 minutes, then add 1 lb. orange slice candy, boil till melted or thick.
   –– Wmrs. William H. Schwartz, Geneva, Ind.

EASY CANNED RHUBARB

Wash and cut rhubarb in desired lengths. Pack tightly in sterile jars. Fill to top with cold water and seal. Do not process at all. This rhubarb is just wonderful for pies. Just open, drain, add sugar, flour and nutmeg, orange flavoring and bake as you would a fresh rhubarb pie.

STRAWBERRY BUTTER

1 - 10 oz. pkg. thawed frozen berries, or fresh
½ lb. soft sweet butter   1 cup powdered sugar

    Have ingredients at room temperature. Blend until completely smooth. Chill.

STRAWBERRY JAM

2 qts. strawberries   2 c. cr. pineapple   13 c. sugar

    Boil 3 minutes, then take off stove and put in ½ bottle Certo. Stir 5 minutes. Then put in jars and seal.
    —— Mrs. Joe B. Byler, N.W., Pa.

HOMEMADE SOAP

    Dissolve 2 cans lye in 7 pints cold water. Let cool, add 10 lbs. lukewarm grease and stir until set. Cut in squares.

FINGERPAINTING PAINT

½ c. Argo stach (corn)   1 c. cold water   1 env. plain gelatin
2 c. hot water   ½ c. soap flakes or detergent
Food coloring

    Combine corn starch and ¾ c. cold water. Soak gelatin in remaining cold water. Stir hot water slowly into corn starch mixture. Cook and stir over medium heat until mixture boils and is clear. Remove from heat, blend in softened gelatin. Stir in soap or detergent until dissolved. Cool mixture, then divide into a jar for each color. Stir food color into mixture in each jar to desired intensity. Cover jars to store.

    When using, have a spoon for each jar. Paper with a coated surface such as glazed shelf paper or butcher paper Sponge and water for wetting paper. Newspapers or oil cloth to protect work area.
    —— Mrs. V. J. Shetler

"The circumference of a blessing cannot be small if God be the center"

AMISH PHILOSOPHY

MOTHER'S Recipe

"Add compassion by the spoonful,
   In the batter of a cake,
Makes it come out light and fluffy,
   Just the finest you can make."

Now these things can't be purchased
   In the store across the way;
But mother keeps them in her heart
   And uses them each day!

MY KITCHEN PRAYER

May the meals I prepare
Be seasoned from above
   With thy Blessing
   And thy Grace
And most all thy love.

"Intelligence is the ability to learn how to learn."

"Of all the hard knocks in life, the hardest to hear is the knock of opportunity."

"It's always a great shock when the apple of your eye turns out to be rotten to the core."

"The Bible is the window in this prison of hope through which we look into eternity!"

INDEX

Cakes, Cupcakes, Coffee Cake	Page 5
Pies	Page 16
Cookies	Page 27
Desserts, Puddings, Ice Cream	Page 39
Candy & Frostings	Page 44
Breads, Rolls, Pancakes	Page 51
Meat & Main Dishes	Page 60
Soups & Casseroles	Page 70
Salads, Pickles, Relishes	Page 78
Jams, Jellies & Miscellaneous	page 86

An attempt has been made to list recipes within a group in alphabetical order, although slight variances to this rule were made to avoid splitting a recipe due to paging. Also, a recipe might be listed under more than one letter. For example: If you do not find Sweet Pickles listed under S, you may find them under P. Some recipes could have been listed under more than one grouping, so if you do not find it in the first place you look, try another grouping.

www.ingramcontent.com/pod-product-compliance
Lightning Source LLC
Chambersburg PA
CBHW061804070526
44586CB00023B/2701